The Collectors:
Dr. Claribel
and
Miss Etta
Cone

Miss Etta Cone by Matisse

14.7.22

Dr. Claribel Cone by Picasso

The Collectors: Dr. Claribel and Miss Etta Cone

by Barbara Pollack

with a "portrait" by
Gertrude Stein

THE **BOBBS-MERRILL** COMPANY, INC.
A SUBSIDIARY OF HOWARD W. SAMS & CO., INC.
Publishers • INDIANAPOLIS • NEW YORK

For Merrill Pollack and William Raney

Library of Congress Catalog Card No. 61-9937

Contents

I am by practice and instinct a collector, and it is the nature of collectors never to feel that enough is as good as a feast. On the contrary, to us even a feast is never quite enough. We may be surrounded by a thousand treasures and yet mourn for a missing one as if we possessed no other.

> Doris Langley Moore
> *The Great Byron Adventure*

Do you know what a collector means to a painter?

> David Lan Bar
> Paris, May 1960
> in conversation with the author

One

Baltimore:
The Steins

WHAT TO DO with daughters has always been something of a problem, unless they are so pretty or so passive or so wealthy that they are snatched up as brides as soon as they come of marriageable age. With Helen and Herman Cone, the problem could have been worse. Of thirteen children born to them, only three were girls.

Herman Cone arrived in the United States from Altenstadt, Germany, in 1846 when he was seventeen. He was fortunate in having a married sister in Richmond, Virginia, which made the new country less terrifying for the gentle boy. Possessing the accepted German virtues of thrift and diligence, Herman did not think about taking a bride until he was twenty-seven, when he was co-owner, with a cousin named Adler, of a country gro-

cery store in Jonesboro, Tennessee. He courted small,
sweet Helen Guggenheimer. She also was German born
and with her two sisters and five brothers had resettled
in Natural Bridge, Virginia. On September 25, 1856,
they were married. Although Helen was nearly ten years
younger than Herman, they made a compatible couple.
Less than a year later nineteen-year-old Helen presented
her husband with a son. The parents named the infant
Moses. It was a good choice for a man destined by nature
and family position to be the leader of a tribe.

In the next twenty-one years Herman and Helen Cone
had nine more sons and three daughters. In their parents' minds the Cone children fell into two groups, one
senior, the other junior. Those born before Albert—
who lived only three months after his birth in 1866—
were always regarded by the family as senior members.
As such, they were addressed by their younger siblings as
"sister" or "brother." After Moses came Ceasar in 1859
(the family chose to alter the usual spelling), Carrie in
1861, Monroe in 1862, and Claribel in 1864. Monroe
died in 1891 at the age of twenty-nine. The junior group
began with Solomon in 1868, then Sydney in 1869, Etta
in 1870, Julius in 1872, Bernard in 1874, Clarence in
1876, and Frederick in 1879.

Moses, Ceasar, and Claribel were the ascendant ones,
the ones who could do anything. Absolutely sure of themselves, each was aggressive, charming, dignified, easy in
manner, never flustered, never at a loss. The younger
seven remained juniors no matter their ages. In their
individual ways they lived out their lives harboring feel-

ings of inferiority. Of the seven, Julius was the most successful in overcoming this difficulty.

The German-Jewish families that settled in the South in the middle of the nineteenth century shared certain characteristics. Like Herman Cone, many of the men spent their first years in America as peddlers, walking from town to town. Purchase of a horse and wagon was the first sign of success. Once children were born, the families settled in small towns and cities and opened small dry goods or haberdashery stores. These German immigrants had the highest expectations for their American-born children. College was not thought a necessary background for a determined youth. It seemed more pertinent for a young man who wanted to get ahead to go to work at fifteen and learn a trade from the bottom up. Still, there was no greater joy for these intellect-loving Germans than to see a son become a professor or a doctor; that advantage was usually saved for a younger son, who might have his financial lot made easier if his elder brother had already begun to make his fortune as a "self-made man."

Such possibilities applied only to sons. There was no future for daughters other than a successful marriage—that is, marriage into another German-Jewish family, preferably of somewhat higher social and financial standing than one's own. Those girls who had not married by the time they were twenty-five were considered confirmed spinsters, supported by their fathers, and expected to keep house for their parents after their presumably luckier sisters had left home.

Herman and Helen Cone lived with their growing family in Jonesboro until a few years after the Civil War. The war did not affect their lives markedly since Herman availed himself of the general custom of hiring a substitute to serve in his place. By the early 1870s both the Cone and Adler families had so multiplied that it was difficult to support them comfortably with profits from one country store. Herman decided to sell his share and move his family to Baltimore, where his wife had many relatives. Shortly after the birth of Etta the Cones made the big move. Claribel was then a plump, curly-haired brunette of six, Moses a sturdy, ingratiating thirteen-year-old.

Baltimore in the 1870s was a city of more than 200,000, and growing fast. Its fashionable homes were clustered around the spacious green promenades of Mount Vernon Place, under the surveillance of a statue of George Washington. The new families in Baltimore were settling a distance away from this older, eighteenth-century part of the city. In a northwesterly direction from Mount Vernon Place was wide, pleasantly landscaped Eutaw Place. Herman Cone looked longingly at new, three-story, attached brownstone houses on Eutaw Place, but finally settled for a more modest house on nearby Lanvale Avenue. The older Cone children attended the local public school. Herman Cone opened a wholesale grocery business, which bore his name, at 15 South Howard Street.

The Cones became members of a Jewish reform temple in their neighborhood. Helen Cone felt strongly about going to a synagogue on religious holidays, but the family life did not center around religious activity. It was, instead, a family in which English was the spoken and written language, in which successful business enterprise and family closeness were regarded as the cardinal virtues. The Cones were busy not only among themselves but also with visiting and entertaining Helen's brothers and sisters, the Guggenheimers, and their children. Herman's business did well. He was soon able to provide his wife with two servants and a seamstress who was kept busy sewing for the many children. He also bought himself a carriage and two horses. Before long he was able to move his family to a more spacious brownstone on Eutaw Place.

When Moses and Ceasar reached their middle teens they left school and began to work for their father as drummers, traveling through the South. In 1878, when Moses Cone turned twenty-one, his father paid him the handsome compliment of renaming his business H. Cone & Sons, acknowledging his pride in Moses and Ceasar as accomplished young businessmen.

So the first two Cone children fell neatly into place. Carrie's role as the eldest daughter was to find herself a husband and rear a family. Trained to assist her mother in the rituals of kitchen, parlor, and linen closets, she helped manage a household of fourteen. Although Carrie had a bright mind and preferred a book to a dustcloth, she was not one to shirk duties. She helped her mother in every way she could.

15

In the spring of 1882 a great event occurred in the Cone household. With Moses able to take care of the prosperous business and Carrie in charge of the household, Helen and Herman Cone felt they could be spared long enough to make a trip to visit their families in Germany, as well as "do" the continent in a sort of belated Grand Tour.

On the day he sailed Herman Cone wrote his children, "I feel perfectly satisfied that you will all know how to manage and take care of the business as well as of home and the younger ones and I also feel satisfied that the younger ones will do the bidding and mind their older Brothers and Sisters." The patterns of early childhood yield reluctantly to time. Forty years later the younger Cones were still "minding" their older brothers and sisters.

In Altenstadt, where Herman's family still lived, the couple were handsomely received, gifts were exchanged, huge dinners were served to honor the visitors. Letters crossed the Atlantic in both directions, the children, all twelve of them, dutifully writing to their parents. Earlier, while Moses and Ceasar were traveling as drummers, the younger children had been encouraged to write to the boys by being paid a nickel a letter by their father. They were good letter writers, as were their parents. A four-page letter was considered a note, an eight-page letter was described as "brief." Ten pages or more verged on respectability. Mother Helen always referred in her writings to "dear Moses" and "dear Ceasar," forms she used as rigidly as "Brother Moses" and "Sister Carrie." Moses used an abbreviation of her form in his letters, referring, in his large, flowing handwriting, to "d'ma" and "d'pa."

The Cones also stopped at Helen's birthplace, Huerben, then went on to Munich where they were met by more relatives. After taking the baths and traveling farther through their native land, they stopped in Paris where Helen shopped for clothes, and then continued to London, which they found "dreary and not at all enjoyable." On September 1 their ship arrived in New York harbor. They had been gone about four months.

When the Cones reached Baltimore they had gifts for all the children and for a long list of cousins and aunts and uncles. They were asked over and over again by homesick relatives to describe the scenic wonders of the trip. Castles and museums, snow-topped mountains, picturesque villages, and family reunions were table talk in the Cone household for months. Claribel undoubtedly compared the images evoked by these stories with what she saw around her in Baltimore. To twelve-year-old Etta, Europe sounded like a wonderful never-never land where everything was friendly, artistic, and refined. Whatever it was like, it certainly didn't sound like Baltimore, and although Etta thought she would always love Baltimore best because her family was there, Europe sounded infinitely inviting.

When, in 1883, Carrie became engaged to Moses Long, a young man living in Baltimore, everyone felt it a great joy and a just reward for a fine girl. It was not considered

17

a brilliant match by the family, but a good one. After all, Carrie was to be married, which left only two unmarried daughters, and that counted for a great deal.

Soon after the marriage Claribel claimed attention by graduating from Western Female High School. Her mother nurtured hope that the family would soon celebrate another betrothal, for Claribel was now nineteen. At the same time Helen Cone was aware of the standards of the day. Eligible young ladies should be dainty, pretty, and alert; not too bright or argumentative; cheerful and demure; not too fat, not too thin, and, at the very least, anxious for marriage.

Claribel Cone failed on every count. She was too plump, much too bright, and much inclined to argue with gentlemen; her waist was not particularly slender, her feet were big. She had a way of standing very straight, which was hardly demure. She spoke with an authority unbecoming a young unmarried woman, supposed to have been trained to at least an appearance of modesty.

Claribel worried her family on other counts. She was invariably late and had a highly vocal detestation of all womanly tasks. She had always resisted being taught to cook and sew and dust and embroider. She refused to step into Carrie's place, yet made demands on the household just as if she were a wage-earning man, not an unmarried female.

What did she like? She enjoyed reading and writing. She studied botany, taught it to a cousin, and then proceeded to learn German. She played the piano nicely and painted pleasant water colors. Yet, for all the confusions

she engendered in her family, her charming smile, warm
sense of humor, and melodious voice redeemed her. If
she could have her own way, if she could come and go as
she wished, if no one argued with her, Claribel was a
delight. Thirteen-year-old Etta, who always addressed
her as Sister Claribel, worshiped her. Tall, big-boned,
earnest Etta often sat silently while Claribel told a visiting gentleman that he was wrong, *quite* wrong, and she
would be happy to enlighten him as to what was really
the case at hand.

Her worried parents sent nineteen-year-old Claribel
to Atlantic City to stay at a properly fashionable hotel
where she might meet the right young man. But Claribel's letters home that summer of 1883 were hardly re-
assuring: ". . . today, for the first time, I succeeded in
rising early and taking a stroll, which was enjoyable because I was entirely alone with my book and the
ocean. . . ." Or, ". . . as to real nice people I have met few.
There is a scarcity of gentlemen, a profusion of ladies,
hence a splendid chance for any man who wants to be
appreciated."

Returning home, Claribel found efforts in her behalf
renewed. She was urged to join the Sociables, a group of
young unmarried men and women who were considered
suitable for each other by their elders. She joined, but
she contradicted the young men—charmingly, of course.

When it was thirteen-year-old Etta's turn to study at
Western Female High School, she wrote an essay about
Florence, Italy, in large, neat, open, modest handwriting.
"Florence," she wrote, "which was formerly the capital

19

of Italy, is situated in the central part of that country. This city is adorned with numerous statues, among which is Michel Angelo's unfinished group, representing the entombment of Christ. Michel Angelo was a painter, sculptor and architect, he contributed largely to the beauty of Florence, and his works may be found throughout the city."

Since nothing was happening to Claribel in Baltimore, her father took her abroad in the autumn of 1886. The twenty-two-year-old girl spent part of the winter in Munich, and in honor of her visit her cousins, the Rosengarts, named their infant daughter Irma Claribel.

After her return Claribel announced one night that she had decided to enter medical school and study to become a doctor. Her parents were shocked. Moses and Ceasar and Carrie and Monroe had moved into their proper niches so easily, and here was Claribel standing firm, declaring in her lovely, musical voice that she was going to study medicine. At first her father tried to discourage her, then was frantic enough to suggest she go to Europe and study art, which he considered the lesser of two evils. But all Claribel wanted to do, she repeated, was enroll at the new Women's Medical College in Baltimore and take the three-year course required for a license to practice.

When Claribel first fixed on becoming a doctor, Women's Medical College in Baltimore was five years old. Incorporated in February 1882 by four male doctors, it was the fourth medical school in the United States where women could study and the first in the South. The first medical college in the world devoted to the education of women physicians, Women's Medical College of Pennsylvania, was then only thirty-seven years old. The first woman to graduate in medicine in Baltimore was Anna Louise Kuhn. A graduate of the same high school Claribel attended, she completed her training at Baltimore Medical College in 1883. It was very much a novelty in the 1880s for women to become doctors and was considered very bluestocking. It automatically indicated one's abdication from the eligible marriage lists.

Since it was obvious that Claribel had little interest in marriage, the family was soon resigned to having a lady medical student in their midst.

Claribel's choice of profession seemed daring merely because it was unconventional. She was not a social crusader or a militant struggler for the "rights of women," nor was she determined to succor the poor. She correctly envisioned other compensations and pleasures for herself. She would enjoy the intellectual stimulation of her studies, she would enjoy her male instructors, she was delighted to be safely away from domesticity. It never occurred to Claribel, as it did to many of her contemporaries, that in her new station in life she should divest herself of feminine frills and fripperies. So off she went in the fall of 1887 to her studies at the small, meagerly equipped Women's Medical College, carrying her lunch wrapped in violet paper and tied with a violet ribbon.

While Claribel was busy with her medical studies, her

two elder brothers were developing a new business enterprise. As drummers for their father's grocery business, the two had traveled to crossroads stores throughout the South, selling flour, coffee, tobacco, and other staples. They learned a great deal about the operation of the Southern cotton mills, since they sold to mill stores; sometimes they accepted cloth in payment for their goods. By the late 1880s, competing wholesalers in the deep South were cutting sharply into Herman Cone's business. In 1888 the grocery firm was sold. Herman Cone, who suffered from heart trouble, who had worked hard in America for over forty years, lent his elder sons the money realized from the sale of the grocery firm and retired. In return the sons paid their father interest on the loan, plus a living allowance.

In its own way Moses Cone's undertaking was as daring as his sister's. Thirty-one-year-old Moses and twenty-nine-year-old Ceasar set out to persuade forty-four mills in the South, then making a light, cheap fabric known as "Southern plaid," which sold for less than a dime a yard, to sell their total output exclusively to the Cones' new commission selling house in New York: Cone Export and Commission Company. Out of the forty-four, only six could resist the persuasive Moses Cone.

The commission selling house was a good way to get into the mill business. The Cone brothers soon found themselves in the business when two mills which had taken cash advances from them were unable to meet their debts; the Cones took over the mills. Later, when two other mills were on the verge of bankruptcy, the brothers took over and kept them operating. All this suited Moses perfectly. During the years when he traveled the dusty roads of the South by wagon, it had been borne in on him that whoever brought the milling and finishing activities to the cotton fields would make a fortune. At that time nearly all cotton was sent to New England mills for finishing. Since Moses Cone wanted to make a fortune, he settled on cotton mills as his means. He also settled, in 1888, on a life's companion, marrying Bertha Lindau, one of the members of the Sociables.

The business exploits of the brothers thrilled but did not surprise the Cone family. They had expected the exceptional from Moses. They were proud, too, that everyone called Claribel "Dr. Cone." It certainly sounded better than Miss Cone.

In 1890 Etta Cone was twenty. She fell heir to Carrie's duties and became her parents' housekeeper. Etta was warm with friends, extremely reserved with strangers. She was five feet six inches tall, a few inches taller than Claribel. She had in common with Claribel large hands and feet. Her earnestness, awkwardness, and shyness were accentuated in a group when Claribel, the charmer, held the attention of all with her enthralling voice and witty conversation. The parents had failed with Claribel, but they were hopeful a husband would be found for Etta. She was encouraged to entertain little groups of friends that included eligible young men; occasionally a reluctant brother would be asked to escort her to local balls. But nothing came of it—no romances bloomed for Etta. And even if any had, it is doubtful whether Etta

23

would have accepted a proposal. Her ideal was her brother Moses. Whatever he said was wonderful, whatever he did miraculous. No mortal could compete with the image she built of Moses. He reciprocated her affection by advising her on various matters. Moses had been the acknowledged "director general" of the Cones for quite a while now. Others in the family occasionally opposed his will—Etta never.

If Etta did not dream of opposing Moses, others of the tribe tried. Sol, who was philosophic by nature and had a keen mind, had been temporarily banished to Asheville, North Carolina, for his rebellious behavior at the age of fifteen. His father found a spot for him as a clerk in a dry goods store. It was thought by Brother Moses and his parents, or at least by his father, that having a job and living in a strange boardinghouse would have a sobering effect on him.

Sydney was next in line and Brother Moses was keeping an eye on his development because he felt that, since the two oldest sons were businessmen, some of the younger ones should be professional men—doctors or lawyers.

After Etta came Julius, who had a strong rebellious streak in his nature, in contrast to his three docile younger brothers. Julius was not sent away from home at the age of fifteen—he ran away and took a job in a North Carolina mill. It did not take his family long to find him and bring him home.

Bernard was a bright boy; Brother Moses thought he might be the family's candidate for the law.

The youngest boys, Clarence and Frederic, were still children. But that was no real explanation for their acute shyness. Frederick, who had been raised by what amounted to two or three sets of parents, real and substitute, had always been a gentle, retiring child, and it did not seem likely he would change.

Shortly before the Cones moved to Baltimore the city had entered on a period of cultural energy. In 1866 the Peabody Institute Library was opened to the public. Its founder was a banker, George Peabody. Born in New England, he had lived in Baltimore long enough to make a fortune and some devoted friends. The library was an advance for Baltimore; it was intended primarily for scholars, but Peabody also instructed the trustees of his $1,400,000 endowment to provide for the general public by establishing a lecture series to be given by "accomplished scholars and men of science." A subscription for a course of forty lectures cost five dollars. During the season of 1871–72 James Russell Lowell lectured on Spencer and Milton, there were lectures on Greek and Egyptian art, Chinese civilization, progress of the human race, and to climax the series, Ralph Waldo Emerson discoursed on inspiration and poetry. One year the series included lectures on Dante, Homer, Pompeii, and the great British orators, as well as such subjects as "Popular Errors as to the Law of Marriage and Divorce" and "Two Illustrated Lectures on the Oyster."

Mr. Peabody also directed his trustees to establish a musical conservatory, which opened in 1868 with 150 pupils. The standards were high; free scholarships were available to public school students.

In 1873 a fine arts exhibit was held at the Peabody Institute. Plaster casts of Classical and Renaissance sculpture were shown. Baltimore's most famous sculptor, William Rinehart, sold the Peabody its first original work—a marble statue of Clytie. In 1881 the Peabody Art Gallery was opened, the first fine arts museum in Baltimore.

The high aims of the Peabody Institute were reinforced further in February 1876. In the Academy of Music, which had been its first music building, the new Johns Hopkins University held the inauguration of its first president, Daniel Coit Gilman. The new university, endowed by another rich merchant, Johns Hopkins, was to be unlike other American colleges in that it had no undergraduate students. It began with a graduate school of arts and sciences and its carefully selected faculty was said to be equal in academic stature to any in European universities. The first location of Johns Hopkins was on Howard Street within walking distance of the Peabody Library. The Peabody Library building, erected between 1875 and 1878, was a unique structure of six stories enclosing an airy central hall. The books were kept on open shelves and the rails on each floor were elaborately ornamented.

Another ten years passed and the excitement increased. Baltimore was gaining national fame as a mecca for young scholars and scientists. Enoch Pratt had founded a public library which, by 1890, owned more than 200,-000 volumes. The Walters Art Gallery, a great private art collection, was occasionally open to the public.

Baltimore had progressed greatly since the 1850s. Then it was the only leading city in the United States without a university, a public library, a conservatory of music, or an art museum.

All of this, of course, was of benefit chiefly to those educated to an appreciation of the arts and sciences.

But the common man was having his adventures too—in 1880 the city observed the hundred and fiftieth anniversary of its founding with a nine-day celebration. Newspapers boasted that 30,000 Baltimore homes were decorated with flowers and bunting and that "a mammoth parade of 30,000 passed under ten triumphal arches, watched by a cheering crowd of 300,000."

In the summer of 1882 Baltimore could boast of its electric lights, and three years later the first electric railway in America was operating between Baltimore and Hamden, a village two miles distant.

It was a time of progress and high-mindedness, there was no doubt about that. Each day the local newspaper included small items that indicated the new spirit:

"KNOWLEDGE SEEKERS" MEETING

At the Thursday evening Meeting of the "Knowledge Seekers" this week the following program was rendered, and proved like the previous meetings, interesting and instructive.

Piano duet—Messrs. Bamberger and Baker
Original Article—"The Advantages of Traveling in Foreign Countries" (Mr. Angelo Hirsch of Berlin and Philadelphia)

Humorous Reading from "Wit and Humor"
Synopsis of Lessing's Play "Emilia Galotti"—Rose
    Goldsmith

Owing to the inclemency of the weather on Thanksgiving night, and in response to numerous requests, Rev. Dr. Joseph Krauskopf has consented to give another reading in December, when he will give an interesting account of his trip thru "Yosemite Valley" and "Chinatown" and will show views of same on canvas.

After Claribel Cone had cards printed announcing her new status, she looked for worlds to conquer and found most of them closed to her. She had graduated first in her class in medical school, and soon after won one of five internships at the Philadelphia Hospital for the Insane, also known as Blockley Hospital. A classmate of Claribel's, Dr. Flora Pollack, also won an internship. For graduates of the small, poorly equipped Women's Medical College to win was regarded as exceptional. Most of the small, now forgotten medical schools of that era—and there were hundreds flourishing throughout the country —were wiped out when professional standards began to rise soon after the beginning of the twentieth century. Those who knew Women's Medical College, founded by Dr. Eugene Cordell and three male colleagues, remember it as a good example of its kind.

In Philadelphia Dr. Cone and Dr. Pollack busied themselves arranging teas for male members of the medical staff. When she had been there only a few weeks

Claribel wrote triumphantly to Etta that her diagnosis of an eye ailment had proved correct and that of the chief surgeon incorrect. She also reported that Dr. Pollack thought her "stiff," a "society woman sort," and that she "put on airs and was affected." Claribel ended her letter cheerily, reporting that Dr. Pollack said she "liked Claribel anyhow." When Claribel asked what the good doctor thought of Etta, the reply was, "Oh, Etta is a perfect child of nature." "Funny," commented Claribel.

Another letter from Claribel, the intern, to Etta, the housekeeper, mentioned a new friend, a young Californian, who with his plump, lively sister had come to live in Baltimore that year. The two, who were orphans, had been sent to Baltimore by their elder brother to live with an aunt, Fannie Bachrach, a sister of their dead mother. Their father's cousins and their mother's brother, the sculptor Ephraim Keyser, also lived in Baltimore. Claribel wrote Etta in January 1891, "I received sweet letters from cousins Flora and Aimee announcing the coming of Leo. May you all enjoy him much—I can't come, you know."

Leo Stein was quite a flirt. He was good company and had many lady friends to whom he addressed himself impartially. So Etta, her cousin Hortense Guggenheimer, and Flora and Aimee all were excited by his presence. They had never known anyone like him. He talked not of money or business or worthy charities, but of art and music and philosophy. His closeness to his sister Gertrude, with whom he shared experiences and ideas, was completely different from the brother-sister relationships these girls knew. Etta loved to sit and listen quietly when Leo held the floor. Leo, though somewhat put off by Etta's painful earnestness, found her a good audience. Just as she gaped while Claribel held company spellbound, Etta now watched the Steins in dumb astonishment: their slouching postures when they flung themselves onto sofas, their loud laughter at private jokes, their hot arguments about paintings, poets, philosophies.

The Cones had frequent opportunities to see Leo and Gertrude, since the Steins had joined a circle of families who all knew one another well, both personally and professionally: The Bachrachs, the Cones, the Guggenheimers, the Franks, the Gutmans, the Bambergers. In the beginning it was nineteen-year-old Leo in whom the Cone sisters were interested. Gertrude, at seventeen, was too young for them.

In 1892 Leo entered Harvard but returned to Baltimore frequently on weekends, during which he spent hours at the Walters Gallery, enjoying particularly the Chinese porcelains and the paintings of the Barbizon School. Leo loved to draw. Pictures were important to him, and he managed to impart that sense of importance to anyone who accompanied him to the gallery.

When he returned to Harvard for the 1893 term he had company. Gertrude found Baltimore a bore without Leo and decided to follow him to Cambridge and enroll at Radcliffe. Since she had not graduated from high school she had to do preparatory work and take special entrance examinations. She was accepted, settled down quickly, and found college life to her liking. Plump, jolly

Gertrude was always available for a hike, a boat ride, a "bum" around Boston. Her hat, invariably askew, and her rumpled shirtwaists were the despair of her more ladylike friends but did not keep most from enjoying her company. It was a good and helpful change for Gertrude after the lonely years of her adolescence in California. Then, books were her only solace, Leo her only companion. She and Leo had been born near Pittsburgh but had spent part of their childhood in Europe. Their erratic father, Daniel Stein, had then moved his wife and five children, Michael, Simon, Bertha, Leo, and Gertrude, to Oakland, California. Left largely to themselves, Leo and Gertrude grew up as best they could.

After her internship Claribel returned to Baltimore to take postgraduate courses in the Pathology Department of the Johns Hopkins Hospital. She boasted to friends that she had tended one private patient while in Philadelphia and that was enough for her. The lab was the place for Dr. Claribel Cone.

The Pathology Building, erected in 1886, was a two-story structure at the corner of Monument and Wolff streets, near the hospital dispensary. The cobblestones clattered constantly as horse-drawn coaches hurried past. The highly regarded Dr. William Welch had been appointed professor of pathology. Claribel settled happily into a regimen of laboratory experiment and association with another male faculty. She also taught at Women's Medical College and became staff pathologist for the small Hospital of the Good Samaritan associated with her school. It was a demanding existence. Surely she had

31

no time to think about a place of her own, so she returned to the family home on Eutaw Place and dumped her domestic needs into Etta's lap.

Across from the Pathology Building, farther north on Wolff Street, a new, three-story, red brick building rose. Set over the entranceway in gold-colored letters was "Women's Fund Memorial Building." Those four words are a succinct summary of the behind-the-scenes struggle to found a medical school as part of Johns Hopkins. The trustees had not succeeded in raising sufficient money. Miss Mary Garrett heard about the money problem from her father, who was one of the trustees. Robert Garrett had made a fortune in the railroad business. Mary aligned herself with three other daughters of trustees and presented a pledge to raise the necessary amount of money if the medical school would be opened from the start to men and women. The women were not to receive equal treatment; they were to receive the same treatment. The trustees huffed and puffed and finally succumbed to the ladies' offer. The ladies, all well-to-do daughters of leading Baltimore families, easily reached their $500,000 goal.

On October 2, 1893, the medical school opened its doors. That first year the school consisted of thirteen men, three women, and fifteen teachers. Though it took another seventeen years, Mary Garrett's insistence on a coeducational medical school in Baltimore sounded the death knell for Women's Medical College. From 1893 on, if a woman wanted badly to be a doctor, Johns Hopkins was the ideal place to study.

Claribel was busy, and so were Leo and Gertrude. The only one who had not progressed to something interesting or enlightening or emancipating was Etta. Good, patient Etta was still at home on Eutaw Place, always there to feed her brothers when they came in from the road; still there, though frowning, when Dr. Claribel sailed in for dinner oblivious to the fact that she might be three hours late; there to be directed by Moses and his wife, Bertha. When Etta did get away from home, it was usually to visit Carrie in Asheville, North Carolina, and bounce her nieces on her knee. Other times she went to Greensboro, North Carolina, to visit those brothers who lived there and were busy with the thriving Cone Mills.

It was Moses Cone who unwittingly gave Etta the means to begin a life of her own. Thus far it has been given over to a variety of unexciting but necessary services for others. By 1896 Moses was doing so well that he wanted to lavish special attentions on his parents. Helen and Herman Cone, living quietly on Eutaw Street, were happy with the constant coming and going of their children and grandchildren. Moses wanted to brighten their plain home. He gave Etta $500 to buy something new for the parlor, leaving the choice up to her.

The money excited Etta. She had handled plenty of household funds, making careful and minute entries in her household accounts of every penny spent for practical purposes. But this money was different—it was to be spent only to make the parlor more comfortable. She knew exactly what she would buy, but confided in no one. She bided her time until Sister Bertha invited Etta to join her on her customary semi-annual shopping trip to New York.

Some months before, Etta had noticed the work of an American painter, Theodore Robinson, in a traveling exhibition at the Peabody Institute. Robinson was born in Vermont, had studied in Paris and traveled in Italy. Later he settled in France, where he became friendly with Monet, which led to an Impressionist approach in his painting. Etta knew he had died earlier that year, at the age of forty-four. In New York she persuaded Sister Bertha to accompany her to a "Widow's Sale" of Robinson's paintings. By the end of the day Helen and Herman Cone, thanks to Etta, were the owners of four Robinson oils. Although Etta could hardly wait to show them to Leo and hear his critique of her purchases, she liked them, and that was enough for her.

Etta's four paintings, when they arrived in Baltimore and were hung in the family living room, left her family dumbfounded. Their shimmering color was a shock for Baltimore, circa 1896. It was not only the appearance of the paintings that rocked the family—it was the news that five hundred dollars of Moses' hard-earned money had gone into paintings, rather than into something useful like a new rug or a sofa.

Etta was perturbed. She had, for the first time, openly gone against family feeling. But her pleasure in *Girl in the Woods, Girl with Violin, Horse Drinking,* and *Mother and Child* turned out to be greater than her distress. As she walked through the house, going about her tasks, she would stop to study each of the paintings.

34

They were duly shown to Leo, who had been away on a trip around the world with his cousin Fred Stein and his uncle Solomon, but his attention was completely focused on his new enthusiasm. Etta had to hear about Leo's discovery.

While traveling in Japan, Leo had become intrigued by Japanese prints. Their astonishing space arrangements, their subtly delineated shapes, their elegant colors excited him. He brought back many examples to show Gertrude and his friends. He also raved about Italy, which he had visited for the first time on the way home. He had traveled to Naples, Rome, Florence, Venice, and everyone had to hear about that. Gertrude had joined him in Europe and the two had spent the summer together.

Thanks to Leo Stein, Etta's world was widening. So was that of the other young Baltimoreans in Leo's coterie. The ladies began discussing plans for their own trips to Europe. Unmarried young ladies found it pleasanter not to travel alone, but that presented no difficulty —there were still plenty of unmarried girl friends in Baltimore to choose from when one needed a travel companion.

That autumn Leo, restless, wondering what in the world he really wanted to do with his life, began some biology studies at Johns Hopkins University. His sister had capped her pleasant academic career at Radcliffe with an irreverent exchange of notes with Professor William James, whom she idolized. When she arrived one morning in a classroom and was handed her examination paper, she looked around the room at the earnest, sweating students, then wrote across the top of the paper, "Dear Professor James, I am so sorry but really I do not feel like an examination paper in philosophy today." She then departed. A postcard arrived in the mail the next day reading, "Dear Miss Stein, I understand perfectly how you feel, I often feel like that myself."

It was William James who urged Gertrude Stein to continue her studies in psychology, which she had begun at Radcliffe with a show of talent. She decided to go to medical school, and where else, if not Johns Hopkins?

The Johns Hopkins University Register for the academic year 1897–98 lists a Miss Gertrude Stein of 215 East Biddle Street, Baltimore, as a first-year medical student. Elsewhere in the same register Dr. Claribel Cone of Women's Medical College, address 1607 Eutaw Place, is listed as taking Special Research.

On those softly hazy Baltimore mornings when Dr. Claribel went to the Johns Hopkins pathology lab, everyone in her family worried about whether she would be late again. Imperturbably, Dr. Claribel emerged from her house in rustling silk skirts, a dark shirtwaist, her dark hair waving away from her pink cheeks into a bun at the nape of her neck. She would float serenely from her house on Eutaw Place to the trolley stop at nearby Lanvale Avenue. Her arms were busy with notebooks, pocketbooks, handkerchiefs, gloves, and lunch containers. The doctor, no matter how late, never seemed in a hurry. She waited until the electric trolley marked Preston

Street arrived, then climbed aboard and settled into a double seat, using the extra one for her paraphernalia. She watched the early morning sights of her city as the trolley made its way from Lanvale to Myrtle Avenue, Dolphin to Argyle, stopping at each for passengers, then continuing on to the next stop, Biddle Street. Then Dr. Claribel would look up to greet her frequent companion, Gertrude Stein, who spilled heavily onto an adjoining seat. After Biddle Street the two rode five more stops to the end of the run at Broadway, then strolled in a leisurely way down Broadway, past interminable small, attached red brick houses, their façades punctuated with white marble steps, hallmark of Baltimore. At Broadway and Monument they turned left. Their destinations were about a half block apart—Gertrude's classes were conducted in the Women's Fund Building and in an adjacent Physiology Building, where preclinical classes were given during the first two years of her medical course. The hospital installation was one street farther, where Claribel entered the Pathology Building next to the dispensary.

Gertrude was struck by Dr. Claribel's ability to tell long, involved stories as they walked. When their paths separated, Claribel would smile and depart without another word. When the two met the next day, the doctor would pick up the story where she had left off. During one of their walks Gertrude accepted Claribel's invitation to speak to a Baltimore women's group. Gertrude titled her rather earnest speech "The Value of a College Education for Women." She painfully typed the speech herself, spending almost as much time correcting the typing as she had in writing the speech.

During these years open house—with Etta preparing the refreshments—was held Saturday nights at 1607 Eutaw Place for Claribel's friends: young doctors, artists and musicians, faculty and students from Johns Hopkins, and, intermittently, Leo and Gertrude. Whenever the Baltimore newspapers wrote about Claribel Cone they always mentioned these Saturday nights. One Baltimore author, Marge Luckett, in her anthology of *Maryland's Distinguished Women* wrote: "Dr. Cone's Saturday night gatherings where the intellectuals of Baltimore gathered to discuss subjects of *Art* and *Culture* are said by the Baltimore *Sun* to be the nearest approach to a salon that Baltimore has." What the *Sun* continued to write was: "Her weekly gathering together of friends more nearly approaches the old idea of the salon than any other drawing-room coterie in the city."

Leo and Gertrude occasionally received friends at their little three-story gray stone house on Biddle Street. Their older brother Michael and his wife Sarah, who lived in California, were appalled that Leo and Gertrude were keeping house. Convinced that neither would trouble with household details, Mike had written to warn against it. But surrounded by Leo's Japanese prints and Gertrude's books and a staunch German housekeeper, the two made out.

Each summer vacation the brother and sister decamped for Europe. After the second summer Leo decided to leave Hopkins and Baltimore to live in Italy and write a book on Mantegna. He never wrote the book, but his absence no doubt made Gertrude realize how little interest she really had in medicine. Nevertheless, she continued, there being nothing else she particularly wanted to do.

Late in 1897 Herman Cone, weakened by a heart attack, summoned his children and his wife to his sickbed so he could speak to each for the last time. After his death it was learned that he had left a modest inheritance for each son and daughter, as well as for Helen. The elder Cone brothers decided to forego their share of the inheritance in favor of their two unmarried sisters, who, it seemed, would never marry. Claribel was thirty-three, Etta twenty-seven when their father died, and even their mother no longer spoke of marriage possibilities. The sisters each now had a private income of approximately $2400 a year.

After Leo left for Florence, Gertrude moved from Biddle Street to share a house on East Eager Street with Emma Lootz, another medical student. Gertrude continued at her medical studies, encouraged a little by letters from Leo suggesting that *somebody* in the Stein family should finish what they had started. His candidate, of course, was Gertrude. He had not written his book on Mantegna. As a matter of fact, he had not even begun it. He was enjoying living in Florence, where there were plenty of pictures to look at.

Around the time Gertrude entered her last year of medical school in the autumn of 1900, travel talk picked up again in the Cone ménage, stimulated by the sisters' financial independence. Gertrude and Etta were not the only ladies in Baltimore who missed Leo; one of Etta's cousins, Hortense Guggenheimer, seems to have missed Leo for reasons of the heart. She and Etta began to talk tentatively of going to Italy together. Leo had written that he would show them around.

As Gertrude's graduation time approached, the usual flurry of official picture taking and unofficial partying occurred. The picture of the class of 1901 shows about four dozen well-scrubbed young men surrounding seven young women of various size and coiffures. A short, heavy-set, frowning young woman standing in the upper right corner, wearing a dark dress buttoned to her chin, is Gertrude Stein. The picture was taken six weeks before graduation; two weeks later it became apparent to Gertrude and the faculty that she was not going to graduate with her class. One of Gertrude's professors, annoyed with her indolent approach to his class, threatened to fail her unless she stayed to make up work for him during the summer. Thankful that the fates had finally taken a hand, Gertrude declined to stay. She concluded her medical career with the following remark to an earnest, remonstrating girl friend: "You have no idea what it is to be bored." Off she sailed for Italy and Leo.

Etta Cone also crossed the ocean to Italy in the early summer of 1901. Her companions were Harriet F. Clark and Hortense Guggenheimer. The three unmarried young women seemed to take adequate pleasure in each other's company—which was just as well, since the customs of the time made it difficult for respectable women to enlarge their circle of friends while traveling. One book of travel hints for ladies printed in 1900 faced the question squarely. Wrote the lady author, ". . . it is not now so unusual as it used to be to see young girls going about alone or together, and, as a general rule, if the woman will dress quietly, walk quickly, and look ahead of her, she will not be molested . . . ."

When their ship docked at Naples late in May, Leo Stein surprised the three ladies by meeting them at the dock. "We almost hugged him with delight," Etta wrote in a travel journal she was keeping. It was a supreme moment for Etta Cone—she had actually crossed the ocean for the first time and was walking the enchanted streets of Naples. Soon she would see Pompeii, Capri, Sorrento, Rome . . . .

Leo Stein liked nothing better than a good audience for his little lectures on art. His new audience, if nothing else, was flatteringly interested in whatever he said, and a little too new to the game to argue. Leo had opinions on many phases of Italian life, as well as its art. And Etta dutifully listened, then noted them in her little journal.

en route from Rome

. . . We saw the women washing in the streams— using the rocks as wash boards. . . . Leo tells us this is a common practice.

Had a unique lunch of veal sandwiches and wine on the train. As usual Leo's talk was far more interesting and fully as expansive as Baedeker.

Many grand sculptures attracted us but Leo had drawn our attention to only the most important.

en route to Orvieto

After an 8 A.M. breakfast, met Leo Stein at the depot and he had a batch of mail for each of us . . . we had an uneventful but warm ride as far as Orvieto . . . we spent the greater part of our stay here at the old Gothic cathedral begun in the 13th century. Leo made us study some large wall frescoes by Luca Signorelli . . . & I found them very impressive. . . . We walked through the town and here we discovered it to be impossible to distinguish between stable and mansion and finally accepted Leo's explanation that cattle and people dwell together in peace and harmony.

We had a ride to Florence with some comical specimens of Italians, one of whom in broken English was very solicitous of my comfort. We passed the time in eating marrons and listening to Leo's charming talk.

Although Leo Stein seems to have done most of the talking about art during Etta Cone's first trip to Italy, Etta retained the right to look at what she liked.

Florence, June 3, 1901—After breakfast at about 10 A.M. Leo came by and took us to the Uffizi Gallery. Here we saw many beautiful Botticellis, Ghirlandaios, Andrea del Sarto. Titian, etc., etc. The Madonna with Child and two angels of Fra Lippo Lippi interested me keenly, as it is so beautiful. . . . I found myself sitting often for thirty minutes before either Andrea del Sarto's Madonna of the Harpies or one of the Madonnas of Botticelli. We walked back to the hotel for lunch which we took without Leo.

June 5 Florence—Made our third visit to the Uffizi and as usual had Leo in his own leisurely way flitting from one to the other of us, each one of us delighted to welcome this wonderful brain. It is marvelous to me to find him absolutely well groomed in every possible field of thought.

After lunch at our hotel and coffee in the Palm Room next to the dining room, we amused ourselves in drawing ourselves on the picture postals of the dining room of this hotel. Leo's went to his uncle Ephraim Keyser and mine I sent to Ida Gutman. Left Leo still holding forth to the girls at 4 P.M. while I came up to rest.— Later we girls had a lone dinner. It was very unique to be the only ladies in sight among a number of men. A very interesting looking crowd.

June 8—Were on our way to the Pitti Gallery and here we passed the rest of the morning in a happy state with the glorious old paintings. Leo Stein joined us and gave us many valuable suggestions. . . . Later, at five o'clock tea at the Steins' friends, the Houghtons, we had a great time playing pitch pennys on Mrs. Houghton's attractive terrace overlooking the Arno, very near the Ponte Vecchio.

June 9—After a late breakfast we three girls made

43

for the "Belle Arti" otherwise known as the Academy. Here we met Leo who in his usual master-like way pointed out the glory of the glories, so we didn't waste time in searching.

By the twelfth of June a shadow of disloyalty to Leo's talk showed up in Etta's journal, when she noted, "After lunch Leo held forth and I came up to rest." The next day she wrote, "After lunch I came up to rest in spite of Leo's attractive talk."

Finally, on June 14, the party rose early and moved on to Pisa, where they went immediately to the cathedral, then the Leaning Tower and the Baptistery. Etta noted in her journal:

> Words cannot do justice to the grandeur of it all. The tower is far more impressive than I had an idea it could possibly be. We walked up to the top of the Leaning Tower and I was not delighted with the sensation. Later, we lay on the grass enjoying the sight of the beautiful buildings until 6:30 P.M. . . . After a very nice dinner we foolishly sat up until after 10:30 P.M. but Leo was very interesting.

Next day they advanced to the medieval walled city of Lucca. Etta noted:

> At the cathedral, Leo explained much of architectural construction to us, of how the arches are constructed, of what a flying buttress consists, etc. . . . Went to a hotel nearby for lunch, and there we were kept prisoners by heavy rain until 5 P.M. We spent

our time variously; Leo and Hortense playing jack straws, Harriet cutting Madonna and Child on back of a walnut shell, and I reading *Little Flowers of St. Francis.*

Back to Florence the party went, and the sightseeing continued, the little flock still dominated by its voluble shepherd. Not for much longer; Leo Stein had been in constant attendance since May 23, and now he wanted to be off. If legend is correct, Hortense's heart would have been affected more than those of the other ladies by his departure. There are those in Baltimore who thought Hortense was in love with Leo, and that she had hoped this trip would culminate, perhaps, in a proposal. So the farewell dinner party when "Hortense opened a bottle of champagne and wouldn't let me pay my half" might have had more nuances to it than Etta Cone chose to notice.

The next day it was all over and Etta duly recorded his leaving:

> Leo took his final farewell at 6 P.M.; he was leaving on the train for Genoa at 7 P.M. We girls made our lonely march to Gambrinis for dinner and missed Leo muchly

Leo Stein's pupil had been well taught. Even without Leo directing her eyes, Etta continued through Italy looking long at the various sights and works of art. By the end of June the ladies had progressed, via Siena and Padua, to Venice. There Etta's journal entry indicates

45

how effectively Leo had succeeded in raising her aware-
ness of painting higher than the tourist level:

> After breakfast we took a gondola for the Academy
> and the first thing that attracted me on going upstairs
> was Titian's glorious *Assumption of the Madonna;*
> next in the same room was my own little Angel of
> Carpaccio in its own place at the foot of the throne.
> These and many others made a great impression on me,
> but on the whole my love for the Florentine school is
> the stronger. . . . Altogether I had a pleasant but con-
> fused feeling after having been at the Academy all
> morning, but hope to get a surer feeling next time.

So Etta already had preferences among the Italian
schools of painting. Also she realized that she could not
appreciate a large group of paintings in one viewing.

Nerves began to catch up with Etta; she noted sleepless nights as the result of becoming overtired while traveling. When she stopped off in Munich to see her relatives, the Rosengarts, Etta found that her developing
standards of art could be a source of friction. One day
she and her cousin Nelly went shopping for antiques.
Etta had already made many purchases on the trip—
some corals, photographs, prints, a book of engravings.
Of her cousin, she wrote:

> I soon found our taste so at variance that I knew a
> task stood ahead. Nelly's taste is less good than conven-
> tional, it is even shoddy though she dresses tastefully.
> After wearing myself out trying to bring Nelly to my
> standard we parted without having made the purchase.

46

After those Arcadian weeks in Italy, where Etta had been lulled into almost continual good spirits by Leo Stein, great art, and the spontaneous warmth of the Italian people, Germany had a souring effect on her. She didn't like the art in Munich:

> We spent the morning at the Glass Palace and were disgusted with the collection, I tried not to let Nellie see for she was so delighted and happy there. The dear hospitality of my relatives was touching, but I am glad I do not live among them.

A high point of each day, wherever the travelers were, was to go to a bank or American Express office whose address they had listed on their itinerary and see if there was any mail from home. Etta's closest confidante at that time in Baltimore was Ida Gutman. The two young women exchanged many letters that summer. Etta had almost a schoolgirl's adoration for her friend Ida. There were no mere mortals in the vocabulary of Etta's affections—there were heroes, such as Moses, and heroines, various women whom during her life she would admire extravagantly. When she was a child she had admired her sweeping, commanding sister Claribel. Feeling always that she was less significant than Sister Claribel and Brother Moses, that somehow she could not win people to her as they did, she tended to exaggerate those relationships of hers which she found at all satisfying.

After leaving Munich the three young women went to Switzerland. Viewing Lake Lucerne, Etta noted that she thought Lake George, New York, was as lovely; another

Swiss resort she found less impressive than Newport. If Etta was tired of scenery, her enthusiasm for seeing paintings never flagged.

She noted in her journal that she was glad to leave Switzerland for Paris. Etta had reached a point in her travels where she was beginning to wonder why she had left home. Her journal records her drooping spirits and then, a pleasant surprise:

> Our arrival in Paris was on time and our search for quarters was interesting—but I fear I wasn't in the mood to enjoy the prospects of living in one of the narrow obscure Paris streets. However, we ended up at the Hotel Quai du Voltaire and found to our amazement that Leo and Gertrude had arrived from their travels an hour before us. Of course we talked a lot—had dinner at the Boeuf à la Mode—it was fine. Coffee at the Café Américain on the Italian Boulevard and now it's Paris with a vengeance.

The flame that had just about fizzled since Leo's defection was soon rekindled in Etta by both of the Steins. Off they went, Etta and Gertrude, to shop for Japanese prints, which their circle was buying that season, thanks to Leo. Seeing the Louvre for the first time also helped to revive Etta:

> . . . the whole place is so redolent of glorious warm color and form that I actually felt enthused once more and forgot any fatigue I had. Our afternoon after we left the Louvre was spent in talk and enjoying Gertrude's charming Japanese prints.

The next days were given over to shopping at the Bon Marché, going to the theater, going antiquing, and resting.

> Got up at 1 P.M. when Gertrude came in with her enthusiasm over her French literature. After lunch we all separated and Harriet and I went in search of antiques and found nothing. We met Gertrude and her friends the Misses Earl buying Japanese prints so we looked hard at some, but held back with might and main.

Etta was finally comfortable with the Steins. She had grown accustomed to them after knowing them for almost ten years. After all, Leo and Gertrude were well educated and had independent incomes. Leo was an aesthete, a very acceptable occupation for a gentleman. Gertrude had no occupation, but ladies were not expected to. Gertrude was excellent, high-spirited company. Leo was cheerful as long as he was the center of lively discussion, able to be the chief speaker. Etta would have been surprised if anyone had suggested there was anything unconventional about her trip or her companions.

To be traveling in Europe was certainly correct enough behavior for well-to-do young Americans. To shop for antiques, go to the theater and opera, to hunt for Japanese prints—none of these activities marked this group as being in any way extraordinary. Etta's journal of the trip records the number of Baltimoreans she met in various European cities doing what she and the Steins were doing.

It had been a long, full summer. Etta grew anxious to go home. It took her all of one night, dark to dawn, to pack her big trunk of purchases to ship directly home. Her days were still busy with the Steins:

> Immediately after lunch I was delighted when Gertrude suggested going to the dressmaker's with me. She was quite amused and interested in the funny conglomeration of French people there. We then wandered along the Rue de la Paix to look in the jewelry shops . . . talked with Gertrude on her pet subject of human intercourse of the sexes. She is truly interesting.

> . . . after a glorious dinner at Marguery's walked home with Leo and had a great talk from Leo on the value of life in a European city and how to regard art.

Like all good travelers, Etta found her funds running low toward the end of the trip. Her minutely detailed account book showed a modest balance. She was watching her expenses carefully:

> Went off to Hayashi's to see his Japanese prints. He has the finest collection in the world. It was a delight and my enthusiasm for Japanese prints grew and grew but pocketbook remained diminished so I withstood them.

When fares of horse-drawn cabs suddenly rose during Etta's last few days in Paris, she noted that detail, along with the expenses incurred when she had to go to various shops to pick up retrimmed hats and silk shirtwaists she had ordered. The night before Etta left, she took Gertrude to the opera, then stayed up late packing her bags to take to London.

Leo took Etta and Hortense Guggenheimer to the depot; Harriet Clark was staying on in Paris. Etta found she was sorry to leave "dear old Paris." By nightfall she and Hortense had crossed the Channel and were on the train to London, their last stopping place before returning home. The two young women spent their first night in London having "a nice long interesting talk on Leo, Gertrude and Europe."

After an uneventful week of sightseeing, Etta and Hortense took themselves to Southampton where they met Gertrude, who had arranged to be on board the same ship. The weary women were finally talked out for the moment.

"Uneventful in every sense of the word," wrote Etta of the second day of the sea voyage. A thick fog enveloped the ship, which put the travelers' nerves on edge. "Found myself listening to the talk and laughter of the young men next to me who have been very attentive in tucking our lap robes, but I fear I am not in a sociable mood," Etta wrote in her journal. "I want awfully to get home."

Her journal ends with the next entry, which reads in entirety, "Clear beautiful day which I spent mostly be low in a beautiful state of mind, but one which brought out the most exquisite qualities of Gertrude. My vanity . . ." A week later Etta was back in Baltimore keeping house for Sister Claribel and her mother.

For the first part of the season in Baltimore, the Cones

had one Stein left—Gertrude. When she returned to Baltimore in the fall of 1901 she planned to do independent research on brain tracts. Soon, however, Gertrude's old restlessness set in and she left Baltimore early in 1902 to rejoin Leo in Europe.

Life continued quietly for the Cones. While Claribel applied herself to teaching and research, Etta concentrated on her family. She had been made an aunt a number of times by her sister Carrie and some of her brothers, and she enjoyed visiting her nieces and nephews in Greensboro.

Moses Cone, who found the Greensboro climate unpleasantly hot in summer, bought land in the North Carolina mountains at Blowing Rock. Both Moses and Ceasar brought their families to summer in the hotel at Blowing Rock. Moses planned to build a large home there.

Brother Ceasar had a bathroom constructed in a wing of the Blowing Rock hotel, which was considered very posh by the other guests. He invited his friends to use it too, but insisted that Claribel use it last, since her two-hour toilettes drove him frantic.

Etta liked Blowing Rock and once persuaded her sister to join her there. Claribel took her microscope, hoping to finish an overdue report. But Greensboro was to Claribel what Baltimore was to Gertrude Stein—a good place to stay away from. Not so Etta. The perfect house guest, she idolized her little nephews and nieces and idealized all the marriages she observed.

One of the family jokes concerned Gertrude Stein,

who once accompanied Claribel on a visit to Brother Ceasar and his wife at their handsome home near the Greensboro mills. Gertrude stretched out on the lawn one afternoon, arms out, eyes closed, to sunbathe. A servant, noticing her, ran to the house screaming, "There's a dead body on the lawn!"

After a spring and summer traveling in Europe, Gertrude and Leo went to London. But London depressed Gertrude and she sailed for New York. She spent the winter of 1902–3 in New York, living with three friends, Mabel Weeks, Estelle Kohn, and Harriet Clark, in a rented house on Riverside Drive which they nicknamed the White House. Harriet, who had toured Italy with Etta, was trying to be a painter, as was Estelle Kohn.

Leo Stein spent that winter in London and bought his first modern oil painting. Writing about it long after, he said, "To have bought an oil painting may not seem like a remarkable thing to have done, but it was remarkable forty-odd years ago for one who was not rich. I had already bought etchings and Japanese prints, but when I bought that picture by Wilson Steer I felt like a desperado. Oil paintings were for the rich: that was part of the American credo."

Wilson Steer and Walter Sickert were the advanced English painters in 1902. As with Etta and her first Robinsons, the great importance for Leo Stein was that he had broken the ice and bought his first oil painting.

Late in 1902 Helen Cone died and Etta was abruptly released from her household duties. The large house on Eutaw Street was now almost empty. Claribel, who had

53

been elected president of Women's Medical College early in 1903, was talking of taking her own apartment. Also she was planning to go to Frankfurt to continue her studies at the Senckenberg Institute.

The summer of 1903 saw another Stein-Cone reunion in Florence, Etta's favorite city. Gertrude arrived a few days after Etta and Claribel. When Etta met Gertrude at the Stazione Centrale, she brought a message: Miss Stein was expected at Bernard Berenson's villa, *I Tatti,* for dinner that night. After her visit at the Berensons', Gertrude returned to Florence from Fiesole and joined Etta in her room for one of their "long talks."

Gertrude tried to tempt Etta to go to Rome with her, but Etta, in spite of her fondness for Gertrude, resisted. Dr. Claribel had plans to go to Germany, and that meant Etta did too. In those days it did not occur to Etta to accommodate herself even if it meant discommoding her sister. Later she discovered the necessity, then the means, to protect herself.

During their reunion the women enjoyed themselves hugely. One of their cousins, Aimee Guggenheimer, joined the party. Etta had begun a new journal for the travels of 1903:

> After lunch we rested and at 5 P.M. Aimee and I took the train at the Duomo for Settignano, where after a twenty-minute wait, Gertrude and Sister C. came, having walked. We four then proceeded to walk to Fiesole and it was a magnificent walk. Heard nightingales for the first time. It was superb. Had a table

d'hôte dinner at Fiesole and all got drunk. Took a cab from Fiesole back to the hotel and sat up as usual talking over the situation. Gertrude is great fun.

Etta enjoyed showing Claribel her favorite paintings. But even more she enjoyed being alone in the galleries, where she sat for a half hour at a time reading her Berenson on Renaissance painters; then she would spend another half hour looking at the paintings for herself. She had become aware of how superficial her first impressions had been. A game she enjoyed playing with herself was to try to determine which painter had influenced or taught which other in the same gallery; often she would have fifteen or twenty of them strung together in her mind in chronological sequence of master and student. After a few weeks it was time for Gertrude to go on to Rome to join other friends, so a last outing was planned.

We took the train, then another steam tram to Saltinis and from there the four of us walked to Vallombrosa. The woods were gorgeous and the scenery all about most ideal. Gertrude was at her best and we were all happy. Aimee made herself known to the little director of the forestry institute and he was most courteous. We went into the woods, overlooking a wonderful valley of pines, cypresses and chestnuts for our lunch. Afterwards Gertrude and I lay there and smoked while Sister Claribel and Aimee went through the buildings, with the little director. Aimee, Gertrude and I then left Sister Claribel to rest, and we took a walk along the most beautiful road. Were sad when we had to wend our way to the depot, for it meant leaving Gertrude. We took drinks at the hotel and then took a tram. Gertrude changed for the train to Rome and we went back to Florence.

The ladies left Florence soon after Gertrude and proceeded to Venice. While in Venice, Etta received an answer to a letter she had written Harriet Cla: ., her companion of two summers ago. "Clark," as Etta used to call her, was living in New York in the White House, where Gertrude had stayed that past winter. "And you are gone to good old Italy!" Harriet wrote. "It is the dream spot of the world and though one mustn't want to live there— that being bad for one's character—I certainly do long to be there.

". . . I suppose you know Leo is painting and gives every promise of being a successful artist. He is filled with enthusiasm and so are his friends. Isn't it delightful?"

Leo's first attempts at painting in 1903 did not produce any great paintings but did cause him to decide to stay in Paris and get a studio. A sculptor cousin of Leo's had just taken a studio in Paris after considerable search. "As I don't like apartment hunting," Leo wrote long after, "I said to him that doubtless he had taken the best he found: what was the next best? He said the next best was 27 Rue de Fleurus. So I settled at 27 Rue de Fleurus."

Two

Paris: Picasso and Matisse

I T WAS THERE Etta and Claribel found Leo and Gertrude, who had moved in with her brother, when they arrived in Paris in mid-September of 1903. After leaving Italy, the sisters had toured, making stops at Munich, Nuremberg, Frankfurt (where Claribel arranged to return for work that winter at the Senckenberg Institute), Amsterdam, and Antwerp.

The section of Paris in which Leo settled was something new to Claribel and Etta; so was being in an artist's studio. Leo seemed very much at home in his new surroundings, as did Gertrude. The former biology student and the ex-medical student had burrowed in with their usual aplomb, and Claribel, never fazed by the unexpected, was delighted to join the fun.

The move, from the Steins' accustomed stopping places in hotels near the Seine to the Rue de Fleurus, signaled the end of their status as American tourists. With a permanent Paris address, with a studio to live in, with their own concierge to scold them, Leo and Gertrude had leaped over the vastness and become Parisians and artists. Their Baltimore friends, who had loyally followed the two Steins around Paris in the earlier hunts for Japanese prints, now found themselves admiring Leo's paintings and listening to his discourses on the stagnation of academic and salon art in Paris.

Rue de Fleurus is a small street off the Boulevard Raspail leading to the Luxembourg Gardens. Farther on, away from the Seine, Boulevard Raspail intersects Boulevard Montparnasse. Crossing Rue de Fleurus at a corner near the Luxembourg Gardens is Rue Madame. The studio Leo had rented was in the rear of the courtyard of the building numbered 27 which faced onto Rue de Fleurus. One got to the studio by passing through the large double gates, walking past the *concierge's* dimly lit apartment, and crossing the courtyard. The Stein establishment had two doors. When going from one to the other it was necessary to step out of doors. The studio, which served as the Stein living room, was through the door at left; the four rooms used for bedrooms, cooking and dining were entered through the right-hand door. Leo had tacked up his Japanese prints in the studio. He did his painting elsewhere. Gertrude had acquired a big Renaissance table and chair. On it she placed her inkstand and piled a stock of notebooks such as French school children use. Gertrude told the sisters she was writing. When Etta asked to see the Wilson Steer painting Leo had bought in London the year before, she was informed it had been put away; Leo now found it too tame.

Etta brought out gifts she had bought during the trip: for Gertrude a lace collar, for Leo a silver paper knife, for Claribel a watch case. For friends at home, Etta had filled a trunk with such trinkets as salt cellars, pepper mills, mosaic breast pins, parchment book covers, parchment picture frames, jade and pearl pendants, an amethyst stickpin, a terra-cotta plaque, terra-cotta heads, terra-cotta paperweights, leather account books, and so on. No item cost Etta more than ten dollars, most cost a dollar or two. All prices were dutifully and individually noted in her personal account book. What could not be recorded was the extraordinary patience it took to pick out all this clutter and pack it for shipment home.

When Etta sailed alone for the United States in the autumn of 1903 she had no idea what her future held. The family home was closed, she had put the furniture, rugs, the piano in storage before going abroad that spring. Why was Etta coming home? What was there for her to do, other than visit family and friends? Habit stronger than reason brought her back once again to the familiar sights of Baltimore and Greensboro, but as the winter wore slowly on, Etta longed for spring and Italy. Claribel was in Frankfurt for the winter; her letters to Etta glowed, telling of her new love affair with the German people, their culture, their cities. Claribel seemed to have love in her heart for everything German; not so her sister. Italy was Etta's playground; or Paris, now that the Steins had set up shop there. Etta learned that Gertrude had come back to America for the winter of 1903–4. The two friends corresponded and made plans to return to Italy together in the spring.

When Gertrude and Etta were ready to sail early in June 1904, Claribel wrote from Frankfurt that she had arranged for their brother Bernard, who was then studying at Columbia University in New York, to have fresh grapefruit sent aboard ship for Etta and Gertrude. "I told him not to have it dressed up fancy," Claribel wrote her sister, "just to have it sent plain so you can have the dressing done from day to day. I sincerely trust your ocean trip may be a comfortable one—that the captain and the pasengers will be 'nice' and that you may enjoy it to the utmost.—Also Gertrude (this may be taken in both ways.)"

Claribel wrote Etta a little about her life in Frankfurt: "I rose before six this morning, after retiring the night before at nearly one—and was in the laboratory before nine. We had a visitor—in fact a whole bunch of them. The chief of them was his excellency somebody or other—I never remember the German names—who is the president of the district, which means that he has jurisdiction over all the institutions of learning in a certain district including Frankfurt. Well, we were all in our places by nine o'clock when this bunch of gentlemen with high silk hats came in—most of them looked rather important—But here it is getting dark.—I will finish this in a day or two." Claribel never did. She had a way of stopping a story in a letter to Etta wherever it suited her—often right in the middle.

Chronically behind in her work, Claribel nevertheless managed a heroic effort to catch up and get off in time to meet Etta and Gertrude in Genoa when they landed there in the last week of June. The party proceeded to Florence, and Gertrude went up to Fiesole to join Leo, who had recently arrived from Paris and rented a villa. Claribel and Etta stayed in the city at the Hotel Helvetia.

Leo had no time that summer to squire ladies from Baltimore around the museums of Florence. In fact he spent very little time at the Uffizi and Pitti. He was on to something new.

During the preceding winter in Paris, Leo had talked to Bernard Berenson, complaining how dull he found the art in the official salons and the big galleries in Paris. Berenson asked Leo if he knew of Paul Cézanne. Leo Stein had never heard of him; he wanted to know where he could see his paintings. Berenson told him to go to the dealer Vollard.

When Leo settled in Fiesole for the summer, Berenson informed Leo that an American heir to a department-store fortune, Charles Loeser, who lived in Florence, owned a number of Cézannes. Leo was puzzled—he had met Loeser casually and visited the villa, noting Loeser's collection of armor, museum-piece furniture, and Renaissance paintings, but he had not noticed any Cézannes. Berenson explained that Loeser kept them tucked away in his bedroom and dressing room. After Berenson arranged a proper introduction, Leo spent day after day studying Loeser's Cézannes.

There is nothing to indicate that the Steins introduced the Cones to Bernard Berenson that summer, or any other summer, for that matter. Through Berenson, the Steins had met Bertrand Russell and the novelist Irsael Zangwill in London. The Steins introduced the Cones to their friends when it suited them, and, as Gertrude Stein used to say, when not, not. This kind of compartmentalized living was very pleasant for the Steins. Friends would turn up from Harvard days, from Baltimore days; friends from New York and Paris would come and then go away and others would come. All this delighted Gertrude, she liked a variegated stream of new and old acquaintances around her. As Etta and Claribel had long since learned in Baltimore—the Steins were the Steins. One either took them or left them. The Cones were delighted to go right on taking them, on Gertrude's and Leo's terms.

After four weeks in Florence the Cones set out on a summer tour similar to the one of the previous year. This time they included stays at Verona and Padua on their way to Venice. The high point of the summer for them was at Bayreuth, where they saw a young American girl from California dancing. In her simple draperies, Isadora Duncan, dancing to the elongated crescendos of Wagner's music, moved Claribel particularly.

When they arrived in Paris there were more Steins to

visit; Gertrude and Leo had neighbors. Their elder brother Michael, who was nine years older than Gertrude, his wife Sarah, or Sally, as her friends called her, and their small son Allan had taken a pleasant, spacious apartment at 58 Rue Madame, just around the corner from 27 Rue de Fleurus. It was about a three-minute walk between the two apartments. There were, it seemed, also small *pensions* for rent in the building, and Etta thought she might ask Madame Vernot, the owner, if she had a small flat for a single lady. It needed to be big enough for a rented piano, because Etta, who had been playing the piano for years, wanted to continue her studies.

Etta and Claribel took to the Michael Steins quickly. Sally was a small, dark-haired young woman, excitable and affectionate, who liked to be in the middle of things. Mike tended to be slow-spoken and a little shy. Shrewd investments and considerable ability had helped Mike to realize a good income out of the San Francisco street railway properties inherited from his father. He had also arranged modest incomes for Leo and Gertrude by his wise investments. Sally had been an art student before her marriage and was excited about the possibility of studying painting in Paris. Their curly-haired son Allan, whom Etta proceeded to spoil, was surrounded by doting adults. Although the two Stein ménages were completely dissimilar, the four Steins shared a common passion for painting.

When the Cone sisters stopped by to call at 27 Rue de Fleurus that autumn, they saw a Cézanne landscape

65

which the Steins had recently bought at Vollard's. No one mentioned Japanese prints any longer; Cézanne was the man of the hour for the Steins. Neither of the Cone sisters had ever seen a Cézanne painting before, nor had they heard of the artist until Leo mentioned his name in Florence, earlier that year.

Although Etta stayed on in Paris after Claribel returned to Frankfurt, she, too, left Paris late in October to spend the winter with friends in Munich. Leo and Gertrude were almost too busy to take notice of Etta's absence but occasionally that winter of 1904 they scrawled a note to her. One of Gertrude's letters that winter began:

"You are an ungrateful brute so you are and I won't never have anything more to do with you, telling everybody that I don't tell you any news."

Her letter goes on: "Miss [Constance] Fletcher has begun to work with Sally. . . . I am having corset covers made by the concierge's sister-in-law. . . . Mrs. Wellman almost had a miscarriage. . . . Miss [Mildred] Aldrich writes plays, smokes cigarettes. . . . She is a very interesting woman—she was here for dinner. . . . There's going to be a Whistler show in London in February. . . . The Russians is very bad people and the Czar a very bad man, anyhow it don't seem to me you are so much on news yourself. You haven't never told me about how the girls spend their time or anything, you are very neglectful and not me to say I don't send you news, how could I write so many letters if I didn't send you news, and what do you think has been in 'em all anyhow. How sharper than a serpent's tongue it is to have ungrateful friends, ah me.

Hei Hei Tujai Bei is wild roaring wild, Hei Hei Tujai Bei, don't get wild my friend.

"There that's news for you, ungrateful cuss, that's what you are ungrateful cuss. That's what you are. No news, nothing but it, I do declare.

"Love to Claribel not to you cause you bad. Gertrude."

"I got a dreadful cold in my head and it makes tears in my nose. . . . Kathleen Bruce is making a little statuette of Allan, it ain't much."

The barrage of nonsense from the Steins continued. Gertrude tried to persuade Etta to go to London with her. She wrote:

"It seems a little foolish to spend the whole winter in Deutschland. It isn't any more of a trip to London than going to Blowing Rock and you do that for a few weeks. I got a cold in my nose, in my left nose, everybody has a cold in their noses. Goodbye be a good girl and do everything the way you are told. Yours, Gertrude."

Leo couldn't resist using the empty space at the bottom of the letter, so he scrawled: "Dear Etta, If I should ever get lost and you should ever hear of it just tip the police and tell them that if they look *inside* my shoes they'll probably find me. I'm really very much obliged to you for the trouble you've taken & will show my gratitude if you ever again come to Paris—by letting you cut up some more Japanese books. Au revoir and good luck to ye's. Leo D. Stein."

When Etta sent Leo and Gertrude a box of cakes at Christmastime they outdid even their earlier efforts:

"My dear Etta: The cakes did arrive and dey was damn good, so says us and the Matthewses and little Roger who got a piece. Have just bought myself material for three pongee waists. Shall I have them made or shall I wait for your over-seeing eye what I axed about in my postal. I ain't made up my mind about flannel ones or tan ones. I will wait for thine and the corset anyhow for your advice. Shall I wait to have my pongees made too? I have had my sandals blackened and wears them joyous in the streets of Paris. Tell Claribel will do my duty resolutely when Houghton's come always perviding I don't forget but I won't forget so don't be worried . . . and again many thanks. Gertrude Stein.

"The kakes ayent so wursst even if thay is maid by dutschmans. Leon D. Stein."

Gertrude signed her letter in a fanciful script reminiscent of George Washington's signature. Leo wrote his in fake children's handwriting.

Etta had had her fill of Germany. When the following autumn came, Claribel returned alone to Frankfurt and Etta went to Paris. There was a vacant flat available near Mike and Sally at 58 Rue Madame, so Etta settled herself there, rented a piano, and was pleased to learn that Madame Vernot also gave piano lessons.

When Etta visited 27 Rue de Fleurus that September of 1905 she was impressed by a new painting on the wall, a portrait of a woman by Cézanne. Gertrude, she learned, had been particularly struck by this portrait. There was a story that went with the painting. When the brother and sister told Vollard they had chosen a portrait of a woman, after spending days arguing over which Cézanne to buy, Vollard said that ordinarily he charged more for a portrait of a woman, but with Cézanne it did not make much difference.

Now that she had an apartment, Etta had a chance to explore Paris in a more leisurely fashion than she had as a tourist. With her guidebook in hand—the book was entitled simply *Paris* by Augustus J. C. Hare (who was also the author of *Walks in London, Walks in Rome,* and *Days Near Paris*)—she ventured forth in the afternoons. Sometimes she strolled in the Luxembourg Gardens. ("The Gardens of the Luxembourg," Etta read, "the 'bel-respire' of Paris, as Lady Morgan calls it, are delightful, and the best type of an ancient French palace plaisance—indeed they are now the prettiest and pleasantest spot in Paris. Diderot has alluded to his walks in these gardens, and Rousseau took his daily exercise here, till he found the gardens becoming too frequented for his misanthropic disposition.") Sometimes she hired a carriage by the hour and went shopping. (Her guide book warned: "Those who engage a carriage by the hour should always ask a coachman for his number and keep it in case of difficulties.")

It was a joyous and uncomplicated existence. Etta found time to indulge a new passion: she began to collect laces and books on lace. She delighted in borrowing Allan Stein and taking him for outings in the Luxembourg Gardens, treating him to sweets and toys. Then there were her twice-weekly piano lessons with Madame

Vernot. Etta also attended occasional concerts, she had letters to answer, accounts to keep up, hats to be re-trimmed and cleaned. On and on it might have gone indefinitely if the Steins had not been around.

"It was in the Autumn of 1905; happening to be in Paris, my sister and I were invited to visit the *vernissage* of the Salon d'Automne," wrote Claribel Cone years later. "This was the year of the Manet Retrospective. It was here that I first saw the Matisse paintings and I must admit I didn't like the paintings. Having passed through several of the larger halls, we happened to find ourselves in a small room which had been set apart for the independent group of which Matisse was chief. The walls were covered with canvases—presenting what seemed to me then a riot of color—sharp and startling, drawing crude and uneven, distortions and exaggerations—composition primitive and simple as though done by a child. We stood in front of a portrait—it was that of a man bearded, brooding, tense, fiercely elemental in color with green eyes (if I remember correctly), blue beard, pink and yellow complexion. It seemed to me grotesque. We asked ourselves, are these things to be taken seriously. As we looked across the room we found our friends the Steins all earnestly contemplating a canvas—the canvas of a woman with a hat tilted jauntily at an angle on the top of her head—the drawing crude, the color bizarre. This was *La Femme au Chapeau*."

The honor of buying the first painting by Henri Matisse out of the Autumn Salon has been claimed by both

Gertrude and Leo. Later, Matisse insisted it had been bought by Sarah Stein. A reading of the contradictory versions published subsequently by Leo and Gertrude only further muddies the water. What was really important was that the purchase of the painting encouraged Matisse at a crucial moment in his development; and a friendship was established between Matisse and both sets of Steins. Matisse sold the painting for about a hundred dollars after some dickering by the Steins over the price.

Henri Matisse was badly in need of enlightened encouragement. The newspapers were having a field day vilifying him and the other artists whose works hung nearby: Derain, Manguin, Marquet, Jean Puy, Valtat, Vlaminck, Friesz, and Rouault. The correspondent for the *Journal de Rouen* wrote: ". . . this has nothing whatever to do with painting, some formless confusion of colors . . . splotches of pigment crudely juxtaposed; the barbaric and naïve sport of a child who plays with the box of colors he just got as a Christmas present." Another wrote of ". . . a gallery of pictorial aberration, of color madness, of unspeakable fantasies produced by people who, if they are not up to some game, ought to be sent back to school." Matisse, after he watched the behavior of the crowds in the galleries, was afraid to bring his wife to the exhibition.

Curiously, Leo Stein recorded his reaction to the painting as similar to that of the crowd. He wrote, "The autumn of this year was marked by something that was decisive. Matisse came out from his *pointillisme* with *Femme au Chapeau*. It was a tremendous effort on his part, a thing brilliant and powerful, but the nastiest smear of paint I had ever seen." Still, the educated, searching eye of Leo saw promise in the painting. To the average viewer it was merely a derisive taunt. But to Leo, "It was what I was unknowingly waiting for, and I would have snatched it at once if I had not needed a few days to get over the unpleasantness of the putting on of the paint. One was not yet accustomed to the smears that since then are the commonplaces of technique."

Gertrude wrote: "People were roaring with laughter at the picture and scratching at it. Gertrude Stein could not understand why, the picture semed to her perfectly natural. The Cézanne portrait had not seemed natural, it had taken her some time to feel that it was natural but this picture by Matisse seemed perfectly natural and she could not understand why it infuriated everybody."

So the *Femme au Chapeau,* a portrait of the painter's wife wearing an elaborate hat, somehow was bought and installed in 27 Rue de Fleurus. A few weeks later Leo, then Gertrude, visited Matisse. Then they took Michael and Sarah with them, who bought a drawing. Next the painter and his wife came to visit at both Stein ménages. It was at Michael's and Sarah's that Etta and Claribel were introduced to Henri Matisse.

"Matisse was really intelligent, he was also witty, and capable of saying exactly what he meant when talking about art." This tribute came from Leo Stein, who prized intelligence in himself and a chosen few others. Matisse, then thirty-six years old, was never bohemian in appearance: his beard and his spectacles added to his air of professorial dignity. Claribel and Etta Cone, as well as Sarah Stein, were enchanted with the looks and manners of the new visitor.

After the fuss about the Autumn Salon subsided, Leo Stein bought a water color of circus figures by a young Spaniard from Clovis Sagot, an ex-clown who had become an art dealer. The dealer said the painter was living in poverty in a Montmartre studio. His name was Pablo Picasso.

A few weeks later Henri-Pierre Roché, a friend of Leo's who "knew" everybody in Paris, took Leo to see Picasso. The studio was in an ancient wooden building high up on Montmartre on Rue Ravignan.

Again, it was not long before the new discovery, Picasso, met the rest of the Stein colony and came to 27 Rue de Fleurus. Tall, beautiful Fernande Olivier came with him. The twenty-five-year-old Spaniard, who spoke some French and no English, was quite a contrast to Matisse. Leo Stein wrote of his "indelible impression" of Picasso: "His short, solid but somehow graceful figure, his firm head with the hair falling forward, careless but not slovenly, emphasized his extraordinary seeing eyes." One of Gertrude's lady friends later described Picasso as resembling "a good-looking bootblack."

The first Picasso oil Leo bought was *Girl with a Bouquet*. Unlike their earlier agreement on the Matisse, Leo and Gertrude split in their feelings about this painting. It was cheap enough—Sagot sold it to Leo for about thirty dollars—but the drawing of the legs and feet of the nude shocked Gertrude. Sagot gaily suggested they

73

buy the painting and cut off the legs. No, that would not do, and Leo and he and Gertrude went back to squabbling. But Leo wanted it very badly. He overruled Gertrude and the first Picasso oil came to the Rue de Fleurus.

Before long Gertrude was posing for her portrait by Picasso. When Gertrude went to Picasso's studio, she would sometimes walk from Rue de Fleurus, which took her about an hour and a half. She might stroll down Rue des Saints Pères, cross the Seine near the Louvre, walk down Rue de Richelieu past the Bibliothèque Nationale. By the time Gertrude reached Boulevard Clichy, the cobbled streets slanted into the long hill one climbed to Montmartre. It was about four miles between the two studios.

Sometimes she took the horse-drawn omnibus at the Odéon, which brought her across Paris and up the hill to Place Blanche. It was still a steep climb from there to the little square adjoining the studio where Picasso lived and worked. During the sittings the two would sit quietly, Picasso staring intently at her strong face and stout body, she calmly returning his look.

After the portrait was well advanced, one day early in November, Gertrude asked Etta if she would like to go along with her. They decided to walk and window-shop along the way.

Inside the old wooden building they passed a number of artist's studios, then knocked at Picasso's door. After the greetings were over Etta looked around the studio. She saw a jumble of broken chairs, a battered sofa, and a small stove for cooking. There was not a bare place on the floor; it was covered with litter. The two American ladies were welcome guests—they brought Picasso and Fernande the colored comics from the Baltimore *Sunday Sun*. While the two eagerly opened to their favorite, the Katzenjammer Kids, Etta picked her way around the studio, noticing with mild horror that the litter on the floor included Picasso's water colors and drawings. Holding skirts aloft, she and Gertrude stooped and picked up drawings by the handfuls. The drawings pleased Etta—winsome drooping women, graceful circus performers. It was incumbent on the new guest to buy something, the chief reason Gertrude had invited her. Picasso was poor, the Steins and their American friends seemed to the artists very rich. So a bargain was struck. Etta was to buy a water color and an etching for twenty dollars—one hundred francs. She was pleased with her purchases but found the portrait of Gertrude less than flattering. After they left Picasso she told Gertrude so and Gertrude laughed.

The Steins introduced Picasso to a number of Americans for the same reason. Sometimes they came to his studio. But he met more of them at 27 Rue de Fleurus, where he came on Saturday nights for dinner, after working on Gertrude's portrait. Of these virginal-seeming young Americans he met through the Steins, Picasso would say, *"ils sont pas des hommes, ils sont pas des femmes, ils sont des américains."*

Picasso also did gouache portraits of Leo and his

nephew Allan. Leo's portrait shows the longish beard he was sporting that season.

Others were beginning to come to the Stein studio—to see the paintings and to see the Steins, which meant they listened to Leo as well. Leo could discourse endlessly for his guests on painting and painters. Gradually, "Saturday nights" at the Rue de Fleurus were becoming an institution. The Michael Steins also entertained on Saturday, but their gatherings were more sedate and usually ended earlier. Some habitués dropped into Mike Stein's, to see the Matisse paintings he had been quietly acquiring, then when that gathering seemed to be ebbing away, the visitors trooped around the corner to the Rue de Fleurus, where everyone could stay until almost dawn.

It was Mike and Sally Stein who first took Etta and Claribel to call on Monsieur and Madame Matisse at 19 Quai Saint Michel in their small apartment overlooking the Seine. At the first visit, in January 1906, the sisters bought a drawing and a water color for twenty dollars. Matisse' daughter Margot said long after this visit, "The friendship and buying of the Cones began in 1906, and it was constant and steady thereafter."

What with all the visiting to and fro, Gertrude found it difficult to get to her own work—writing a group of stories. Gradually she came to write only at night. After 11 P.M. she was certain that no one would rap on her studio door, asking to see the paintings. During the day and early evening friends as well as strangers with slight introductions dropped by at any hour. There were many other paintings to see now besides those of Picasso, Matisse, and Cézanne. The Steins owned a number of Renoirs, two Gauguins, Manguins, a small Daumier, a number of Cézanne water colors, a little Delacroix, and a fairly good-sized El Greco.

Working at night solved Gertrude's problem of when to write. She wrote her stories in longhand, as it made her nervous to type. When she did type, her sentences usually came out looking as if they stuttered. A sample: "Nowist he tim eforall goodmento come . . ." After she had corrected the typing, it was even messier looking. Gertrude finished her three stories and read them to Sally, who was very moved. Two of the stories told of German servants in Baltimore, the third was about a Negro girl named Melanctha. But the typing was still a problem. Gertrude later wrote about how she solved it: "Etta Cone offered to typewrite *Three Lives* and she began. Baltimore is famous for the delicate sensibilities and conscientiousness of its inhabitants. It suddenly occurred to Gertrude Stein that she had not told Etta Cone to read the manuscript before beginning to typewrite it. She went to see her and there indeed was Etta Cone faithfully copying the manuscript letter by letter so that she might not by any indiscretion become conscious of the meaning. Permission to read the text having been given the typewriting went on."

In her cozy room at 58 Rue Madame, Etta sat typing the strangely disturbing words of a friend who still seemed the jolly, friendly chum with whom she had shared so many pleasant excursions. As the chill early spring days passed, Etta clicked off the letters which had, only at Gertrude's insistence, now become words and thoughts. . . .

Melanctha now really was beginning as a woman. She was ready, and she began to search in the streets and in dark corners to discover men and to learn their natures and their various ways of working.

In these next years Melanctha learned many ways that lead to wisdom. She learned the ways, and dimly in the distance she saw wisdom. These years of learning led very straight to trouble for Melanctha, though in these years Melanctha never did or meant anything that was really wrong. . . .

Now it was time for Claribel to meet Picasso and see the portrait he was doing of Gertrude. And, of course, it was clearly understood that the finances of the artist could use a boost. So off to Montmartre went the visitor from Frankfurt, with Etta and Gertrude. Again, the comic strips of the Baltimore *Sun* were brought as the chief offering. As before, the ladies investigated the litter around the studio. They found some lovely pen drawings of women and children, young women riding horses, and some more of the circus figures—an acrobat, a violinist. Etta Cone noted the purchases of that day, March 3, 1906, in her account book. Etta really splurged—buying eleven drawings and seven etchings, for which she paid Picasso 175 francs—less than two dollars apiece.

That winter, which had proved a lively one in Paris, had only a few novelties left for the Steins. Leo and Gertrude brought Picasso and Matisse together at their studio for the first time. The brother and sister were not surprised when it turned out that the painters did not take to one another. One day, when Gertrude arrived to sit for Picasso, she discovered he had painted out the head of her portrait. She had been sitting for him almost every day for three or four months. "I can't see you any longer when I look," Picasso said.

Now it was spring, the time when all good Parisians think about going off somewhere for the summer. Only tourists and the honest poor stayed in Paris during the summer. The Picassos were going to Spain, the Matisses to Italy. The Steins were going back to Florence. The Cones were to be busy with family that summer.

Etta had received a letter from Brother Moses in February announcing that he and his wife, Sister Bertha, had decided it was time they took the Grand Tour, and what better guides for such an undertaking than Etta and Claribel, if she were willing. Moses, Etta learned, was not well, he was afflicted continually with headaches and his doctor had warned him that he must get away from the demands of business. A trip to Europe seemed a good way to accomplish the desired break from business pressures. This was to be the first pleasure trip Moses Cone had ever taken.

It was sometime after Moses' letter arrived, and around the time she finished typing Gertrude's stories, that Etta began to suffer from an old complaint—severe

79

stomach pains. Nothing seemed to help and in a state of considerable pain and unhappiness Etta packed her bags, said good-bye to Gertrude, and went off to Munich in April, 1906, to consult a specialist Claribel had recommended.

Three

The Flowers of Friendship

S OON AFTER ETTA CONE left Paris in 1906 the Michael Stein family was upset by news of the San Francisco earthquake and made plans immediately to sail for America, so that Michael could learn the extent of damage to his property in San Francisco. Sally decided to take some art with her, and late in April Henri Matisse's paintings were taken to America for the first time.

Gertrude received a letter from Etta the week the elder Steins left. Etta was living with Claribel on Beethoven Street in Frankfurt. Still bemoaning the ways of the Germans, she complained of the difficulties she had had in sending Gertrude five hundred francs from Frankfurt. Etta requested that Gertrude let her know when and if the money arrived. "Please, if you need more money, say so, for both Sister C. and I are fortified beyond our needs and you know how welcome you are."

Regarding her health, "At last I have been punched and pounded by a doctor, who finds my digestive tract from beginning to end in a nervous beastly condition, and even the old heart is beating time in a nervous way, otherwise I am perfectly well."

The two old friends from Baltimore found fun in their letters gossiping about family affairs of the Stein relatives and Etta's relatives back in Baltimore—and what grist for the mill it was when one of Gertrude's cousins, Simon Stein, began courting Etta's first cousin, Dolene Guggenheimer. References to the lovers darted in and out of Etta's and Gertrude's correspondence. Later, when Dolene and Simon finally married, Etta and Claribel and Gertrude and Leo became distantly related cousins by marriage, thus perplexing forever after those who wrote about the Cones and the Steins. Half of the writers have called them cousins, the other half emphatically denying it. If one can gain a cousin when one's cousin marries the cousin of a friend—well, then the Cone sisters and Gertrude Stein and Leo and Michael eventually all became cousins, albeit in a remote fashion.

Etta pressed Gertrude to let her know if she were going to Italy that summer of 1906, because Etta and Claribel expected to leave Frankfurt for Naples the end of May. Gertrude wrote back, why Naples?

"Why Naples," Etta replied in the middle of May, "because Mike didn't know my eldest brother and Gertrude didn't know my eldest brother and Sally didn't know my eldest brother, but little Etta did know Brother Mosie. Well, sad be my lot, and sorry my tummy and weakly my nerves, but they is all got to go to Naples and that very soon." Brother Moses was on his way.

The experience of typing Gertrude's stories—now titled *Three Lives* and being circulated to publishers— had not been wasted on Etta. Her remarks about her brother were an excellent, perhaps unconscious, reflection of her friend's rolling, roiling sentences. Etta closed her letter with another reference to money: "By the way, don't you need some cash, don't hesitate and you needn't luxuriate in the feeling of poverty, for it's no use to.

"My tummy aches awful so I must stop and hold it. Good-bye with my sister's respect and my love, Etta."

Brother Moses and Sister Bertha arrived in Italy to learn that Etta was still abed in Frankfurt with Sister Claribel in charge. By the middle of June, Etta hoped that her ulcers, which was what the doctors now called her condition, would improve enough to let her join her brother in Paris in July. Etta warned Gertrude that Brother Moses would be arriving in Florence shortly. "Sister Bertha and Brother Mosie no doubt let you know that they expected to reach Florence about Sunday June 17th and expect to stop at the Hotel de la Ville. Guess you know where it is, there on the Arno near the Grand."

The autumn of 1906 found Etta still ailing with what she referred to as her "bum gut," and although Gertrude wrote that she needed Etta and her typewriter back in

Paris, there seemed little possibility of Etta ever returning to her volunteer work. She was completely absorbed in problems of her health and her family. She hoped to be back in Paris by the middle of October, she wrote Gertrude, but "Goodness knows how long we will be there as when I leave Frankfurt I shall no longer be my own boss. Goodbye to little Etta's freedom, but somehow I never did mind being bossed by my biggest brother— don't know how it'll go in Europe. I see you have some misgivings."

In retort to a letter containing Gertrude's gossip about the financial troubles of the artists they both knew, Etta wrote, "Poor little Picasso! but then I'd swap all around with his health and genius, were it possible, but as it is not, I've just got to fight it out to the end and it's not unhappy I've been lately pain & all included and it's not America either that I'm hankering arter. . . . Your details about Picasso were surely pleasure giving and I'm not to blame for not knowing who Fernande was when I never knew that Mme. Picasso even had a first name. Somehow I ain't of the intimate sort with names. . . . Well, adios, with much love and sort of glad at the prospect of seeing you soon even if I can do no typewriting as wants to. Yours, Etta."

Nor would Etta admit she guessed Fernande was not Madame Picasso, even after she learned the young lady's name.

So Etta, for all practical purposes, had rejoined the Cone family bosom. Well, no matter, Gertrude was too wise in the ways of people to have ever really expected her to leave it. Certainly Gertrude understood about women and their big brothers. But that did not solve the problem of who was going to type her new book, on which she had been working all summer in Italy. It was to be a history of all the kinds of people there have ever been, and every part of Gertrude's forces were united in an overwhelming effort to put all this on paper. Leo would not read Gertrude's writing; he had read some of her work and pronounced it rubbish. Picasso could not; he didn't read English. For all her fascinating acquaintances in Paris—the artists and poets of Rue Ravignan, the Americans who were drifting into Paris, those of many nationalities who came to see the paintings at the studio and listen to Leo's lectures on the glories of Picasso, Cézanne, and Matisse—Gertrude Stein was alone with herself and her work.

When Etta reached Paris in late autumn 1906 it was to resume a right-bank existence with her brother and sister-in-law at the expensive Hotel Athénée at 15 Rue Scribe. One of her notes to Gertrude suggests that she felt a little self-conscious about where she was living: "Dear Gertrude: How would Wednesday afternoon suit you to go to the Louvre? If you can conveniently give it up, would you meet us here at two o'clock? I ask you to call here since the Louvre is on our side of the river, and I think we can gain time. . . . If we do not hear from you, we will expect you. . . ."

Claribel Cone sailed back to the United States to put her affairs in some order before undertaking a trip around the world. Moses had invited both sisters to join him and his wife. While in Baltimore, Claribel accepted an invitation from the Arundel Club to speak on "The American Woman Abroad."

She opened her speech by dividing American women travelers into a few major categories—pseudo-workers, the dutiful, and the idlers. Describing the dutiful, she said: "Women who belong to this class may perhaps be seen pacing the long corridors of an art museum following in the wake of some Cook procession, or listening to wise words of some astute young college professor discoursing learnedly on art. . . . Whether professional or amateur, she is working away at her art with an earnestness of purpose and a devotion which would warrant a greater degree of fitness than is sometimes found," Claribel continued. "And so we hear the cry of the artist:

> The dilettante stalks abroad
> The Amateur is loosed.
> The voice of the Aesthete
>   is heard in the land
> And catastrophe is upon us.

Claribel found the pseudo-worker as diligent as the dutiful. She hurried past them both to get to the class that really interested her—the idlers. "The horizon is not completed between the two red covers of a Baedeker," she said. "They may or may not know the maker of a picture before them—but they know that it is beautiful."

Claribel then quoted Robert Louis Stevenson at some length: " 'Idleness, so called, does not consist in doing nothing, but in doing a great deal not recognized in the dogmatic formularies of the ruling class. Idleness has as good a right to state its position as industry itself. It is a sore thing to have labored along and scaled the arduous hilltops and when all is done find humanity indifferent to your achievement. Hence athletes condemn the un-physical, financiers have only a toleration for those who know not stocks, literary people condemn the unlettered —and people of all pursuits combine to disparage those who have none.' "

Etta was busy during Claribel's absence showing her brother and his wife around Paris. They went to see Ger-trude's portrait by Picasso—which the artist had com-pleted without his model in the fall of 1906. Mr. and Mrs. Cone found it a poor likeness. She took the Moses Cones to see Matisse in his studio, and during that fall of 1906 Etta bought her first Matisse oil, *Yellow Pottery from Provence.* There was the inevitable series of visits by Moses and his wife to see the collections at 27 Rue de Fleurus and 58 Rue Madame. Etta was happy when Mrs. Moses Cone unexpectedly bought a Picasso drawing, a pencil study for *Woman with Loaves,* out of one of Ger-trude's portfolios. Every little bit of money helped. Etta also bought her first Matisse bronze that season—a head of Pierre Matisse, the artist's young son.

Then it was time to prepare for the Cones' much-dis-cussed trip around the world. They were all to meet in Vienna in December, 1906, and start their journey from there. Vienna was chosen because Moses planned to enter a sanitarium there for a brief rest before the trip. His

health was still not good. As it turned out, the last fre-
netic weeks in Paris were too much for Etta, and she
wound up in the sanitarium too. There had been a constant round of socializing and packing just before Etta
left Paris. Among the parties was a welcome-home celebration for Sarah and Michael, back from San Francisco.
Sally boasted gaily of selling the first Matisse in America
to frame maker and painter George Of in San Francisco.
At the party Etta met two young American women who
had recently arrived in Paris—slender, dark-haired Alice
Toklas, who was interested in music and played the
piano, and a writer, Harriet Lane Levy. Miss Toklas and
Miss Levy were sharing a small apartment on Notre
Dame des Champs. The young women, both from San
Francisco, had been inspired to make the long trip to
Paris after hearing Sally Stein's descriptions of her life
there, and also by seeing the Matisse paintings Sally had
brought home.

Just before she left Paris for Vienna, Etta heard from
Sally that Gertrude had found someone to do her typing
—the newest addition to the charmed circle of 27 Rue
de Fleurus—Alice Toklas.

By February, 1907, the Cone safari had wended its way
to Shepheard's Hotel in Cairo, and there Etta paused to
answer a letter from Gertrude announcing that now *she*
was having stomach trouble. The Cone party had left
Vienna around the New Year and traveled first to Buda-
pest, then Constantinople, Athens, Jerusalem and on to
Cairo. Etta reported that her health and spirits were

much improved. "Every whit of my oriental blood re-
joices in hot sympathy for these charming people, and
if my brother weren't so dead set against leaving us out
here or in Europe I might be a harem-lady, who knows?

"Our trip up the Nile was most comfy and beautiful
& although we weren't 'Cookies' on a tour, there was a
good deal of being led by the nose after all and that I
didn't love much, but then Brother Mosie and Sister
Claribel were drinking in chunks of information wholesale, in all the Temples and Tombs where our Drago-
man guide of the Hamburg-American house boat took
us, and so Sister Bertha and I could easily play hooky
sometimes and have fun with these gentle, dirty charming folk, the most ignorant of whom are as quick as
greased lightning in comparison with the average German people.

"It's an awful letter I am sending you, but I am most
sleepy after a whole day in the desert. I am most jealous
that it's you and not me what's got a Renoir. Guess I'll
take out my joy in viewing it (happy thought) in your
atelier. Sally and Mike's place must be beautiful. We're
two days behind but I am happy to stay here. Give my
best love to Sally, Mike, Allan & yourself and my respects to Leo and write soon to your Etta.

"P.S. My brother still thinks he has the three nicest
women folks in the world with him, so all is serene and
sweet.

"P.S. Has my successor done her duty by my place
what she usurped and does she your typewriting & takes
she care of that nice Mikey man. I am sometimes envious,

but guess I am greedy, cause so far, this trip has not been at all a bad stunt. It's not Ameriky I am hankering arter and every night my sister says: Etta, I don't expect to like American life. & I lays low and says nothing & only hopes. Mabel Haines sent a awful stylish announcement to my sister & Miss Rutherford's going to get married & she is more than forty and that's all. Again. Etta. My respects to Madame Vernot, Picasso and the Matisses."

Etta failed to tell Gertrude that an English-speaking Sultan the Cones met aboard the Nile houseboat had taken a shine to the ample charms of Claribel and offered to buy her from Moses. Moses declined the offer.

Although the old cliché about travel being broadening is rarely challenged, travel has its drawbacks too. There is less opportunity to get away from familial irritations on an elephant's back or in a houseboat on the Nile than there is at home. It was inevitable that each Cone should run true to type on the trip. Sister Claribel was invariably late. Brother Moses was always impatient with her. Sister Bertha and Etta, as usual, tried to smooth the troubled waters. Etta made friends with the native children and paid them to guide her to the bazaars wherever she went in the Orient, just as she had always done in Italy. Moses wanted to know the dates of dynasties and the size of entombed kings' treasuries. Claribel interested herself in all this, as well as sanitation conditions in foreign hospitals. Fortunately, all the Cones shared one pleasure in common—they were great shoppers. Moses bought some stone Buddhas in India and arranged for their shipment to Greensboro. Etta bought inexpensive bazaar merchandise for gifts. Both sisters succumbed to the fine fabrics, the brass, and the wood carvings. They bought Kashmir shawls in India embroidered all over with people and animals and birds; whole narratives of court life were illustrated on the shawls. They bought gorgeously colored saris shot through with gold; they bought Hindu jewelry. In Turkey they bought dozens of towels colorfully embroidered at both end with roses, carnations and hyacinths.

In Japan they bought woodcuts, ivories, lacquered ware, and textiles. In China, complete imperial robes and ceramics. Daggers, Persian tiles, Coptic fragments— the shipping lists grew longer and longer. They all bought and bought; it was so tempting, the prices were less than in Europe for fine merchandise, and besides, it was fun.

The travelers were aboard ship between Canton and Shanghai when Etta wrote to Gertrude in May. She still missed Paris but said she "was getting so happy over this lovely Chinese country that I feel repaid a bit for having sacrificed a summer in Italy."

Although Etta was never one for coming right out and admitting that all was not rosy within the family circle, she loved to tease Gertrude with hints, such as "I could add a chapter or two to a certain book you were contemplating writing and Brother Mosie could give you some valuable touches, but it's not to be an autobiography so I just won't tell you anything.

"Now do be amiable and send me some good hot Italian breezes to Baltimore, 2326 Eutaw Place, my brother Sydney's home, where my mail must come for the present. My wanderings promise still to be a perpetual motion proposition, for there is no happy home awaiting the Cone Sisters and no prospect of one.

"Good bye. Take much love and get the typewriter in good condition in case—but I don't know. Love to dear Sally and nice Mikey and to Leo if he wants it and to Allan. Yours, Etta."

When the Cones landed in San Francisco it was acknowledged that the trip had been a tremendous success in all respects but one—it had not restored Brother Moses to good health. He had to be helped off the boat, and immediately took to his bed in a San Francisco hotel.

Solicitous of Moses as the sisters were, both were furious with him when he announced in San Francisco that the whole trip was on him. The sisters were frantic at the thought of how much more shopping they might have done *if they had known* they were not to repay their brother at the end of the trip for transportation, hotels, and other travel expenses.

The party lingered in San Francisco a few weeks, while Moses gradually regained his strength. He, too, had been afflicted with stomach trouble, Etta wrote Gertrude, blaming it on the Siberian cold-storage food they had eaten aboard ship.

Etta and Claribel visited Sally Stein's mother in San Francisco. Etta wrote Sally in July, "My sister was so charmed with your mother's dainty exquisitely kept apartment and let me whisper that I think it made my sister a bit desirous for a like shelter for all the trash she has gathered from all corners of the globe; howsome'er no word was spoken and the Cone sisters seem doomed as homeless wanderers still.

"Well, I must quit now and join Sister Bertha in a search for toys and other things to fill in our presents for the family & friends awaiting us and our foreign souvenirs."

After the Cones had been welcomed by their friends and relatives in Baltimore the two sisters parted again. In spite of Etta's hopes, Claribel had not indicated any desire to share a home with her younger sister. Claribel took an apartment at the new Marlborough Apartments on Eutaw Place and Wilson Street. Etta, homeless, accepted the invitation of her brother Ceasar to keep house for him in Greensboro while his wife Jeanette traveled north for her health. But before Etta was allowed to go south to become Ceasar's housekeeper, Claribel assigned her the job of unpacking the furniture and objets d'art they had in storage and furnishing her new two-room apartment in the Marlborough. Etta wrote Sally of her silent revenge: "All I can possibly sell out I shall do on the quiet—it's a silly extravagance keeping all the old stuff." No doubt Etta was referring to the old Cone family furnishings she herself had put in storage in 1903.

Etta's letters from Greensboro to Paris that winter were cheerful enough; she was having fun. She wrote Mike, "Wish you could all come to see me here, I'm boss." Considerable distance between the two sisters was necessary before Etta could become boss. It had never

95

escaped the Steins that Claribel had the Cone family habit of dominating her younger sister when it suited her, and ignoring her on other occasions. But Brother Ceasar knew a good thing and was delighted to spoil Etta and let her boss him and his young sons.

A letter from Gertrude in January, 1908, informed Etta that Mahonri Young, the Mormon sculptor, had married. Etta had met him in Paris, found him quite attractive, and was happily surprised when he was unusually attentive. She had seemed to reciprocate his feeling. Now Etta wrote back, "Gee, don't tell me Young is married. My last hope." She sketched a little face with dots under the eyes and captioned it, "Those are tears."

Gertrude had also forwarded a small sketch by Picasso, showing his round tummy, his hat in hand. The sketch was headed, "Bon Jour Mademoiselle Cone." Etta replied, "Here comes your dear old letter with this delightful sketch of Picasso's and Fernande's nice wishes. Dey am sure nice folk & I hope to see them in the near future, so thank them for their respects and please give them mine and tell Pablo that Fernande ought to massage his tummy into shape again. I love his picture for it is just like him."

Etta was worried about leaving North Carolina. Her beloved brother Moses was becoming more dependent on her; he did not seem to regain his health no matter how many rest cures he took. She wrote to Gertrude in February, 1908, from Greensboro, "There is only one thing weighing heavy on me now—but for heaven sakes don't mention it—to any of my American family or friends—for no one knows but I am awfully depressed about Brother Mosie for he is not well. He seems better right now and if he is in pretty good shape, I shall sail sure as fate on May 2 for I am wild to see you'ns and Italy and all that I love best in the world outside of this tiny little group down here. Your postal with all the nice signatures gave me pleasure and if I don't get back to Italy and Paris soon I'll go crazy. . . . Take heaps of love, and be a little glad to see the tragic Cone sisters loom up some time in June for we stops first in Rome."

Writing to Sally after she had returned to Baltimore, Etta commented on the feuding Baltimore women they knew in common: "Heaps has happened and heaps that's funny and provincial and all that, but I love 'em all and they loves me in this village, so what's the use of bothering about their idiosyncrasies specially since I can come to Italy and you'uns and forget all that's bad and think of de good."

By the end of May the two sisters were in Rome, where they were to stay for two weeks. This was arranged especially for Claribel's pleasure, since she had had to forego a visit there when she was nursing Etta in Frankfurt in 1906.

One afternoon soon after their arrival Etta stayed in her room at the Hotel Eden to write letters. Among the batch she mailed was an answer to one from Gertrude: "It was nice to get a letter from you on this side and I think it's even nicer to have the pleasant prospect of meeting you next Monday.

"Everybody is more or less fun to me these days. Even

my sister is amusing me, and this afternoon I sent her off for the first time all by her little self in a little cab to the big St. Peter's to see the big Pope and I can only say my prayers and hope she will turn up safe here at dinner time."

When the Cone sisters met with their old friends in Florence in June there was a lot of catching up to do. Their last meeting had been in December, 1906, in Paris, and although Gertrude loved to gossip in letters and loved Etta to tell her all the gossip of those they knew in common, there was quite a bit that had never got into the letters. For one thing, Miss Toklas had come to live with Gertrude and her brother in Paris. She not only did Gertrude's typewriting in Paris but accompanied her to art galleries, to artists' studios, to the theater. Miss Toklas had spent the last two summers in Italy with the Steins.

No, Gertrude reported, she had not found a publisher for *Three Lives*. Friends in New York were now recommending that Gertrude undertake the expense of publishing the book herself. Gertrude was still involved in a very long book she had been working on for years. The end was nowhere in sight. Leo said he had stopped painting altogether and didn't know if he would paint again.

And the Picassos? Well, Fernande and Picasso were a thing of the past—or so it seemed at the moment. Pablo's work was taking marvelous new directions—nothing like the delightful drawings Etta had in her portfolios in Baltimore. Very different, Gertrude reported, the sisters would have to see for themselves when they got to Paris.

Leo did not share Gertrude's enthusiasm for Pablo's new work. He looked rather sour whenever the subject was discussed. Picasso had been working intermittently on a large canvas of nude women with strangely distorted bodies and primitive masklike faces, even further removed from representation than Gertrude's portrait.

Just before the Cones left Paris for the Orient, they had seen Matisse's tremendous *Joy of Life* hanging in the Rue de Fleurus studio. Matisse asked the Steins to hang it, since he did not have room in his small apartment, after it had been shown at the Salon des Indépendents in the spring of 1906. All the Steins had bought important new Matisses during the absence of the Cone sisters. Michael and Sarah now owned a *Blue Still Life*, *La Coiffure*, and *The Red Madras Headdress*. Leo and Gertrude had added to their collection a sketch for Matisse's *La Musique* and a painting of a nude lady, extremely distorted, which everyone called *The Blue Nude*. Matisse had painted it after a visit to North Africa. Gertrude told them her *concierge's* son said, "Oh, la, la, what a beautiful body of a woman!" when he saw *The Blue Nude*.

A week after the Cones reached Florence, Michael, Sally, and Allan Stein arrived from Paris. The rounds of visiting and shopping were intensified. The summer went placidly along for the Cones and their friends, but mail from home troubled Etta. As August began, the news from Greensboro about Moses' health, and letters from Brother Moses telling her how much he missed her, so upset Etta that she made plans to sail to America late that month. Michael and Sarah, who felt close to Etta, wanted to accompany her to Paris, but she would have none of it. By September the sisters had returned to America without having had an opportunity to pause for the pleasure of seeing the new paintings of their artist friends.

A letter from Etta to Gertrude, written at Blowing Rock, Moses' mountaintop estate in the Blue Ridge Mountains, dated October 18, reports, "Brother Mosie is in fair shape right now, but I fear I shall always be nervous about him when I am not on the spot. We are here alone right now and between the walks and drives I am busy." Etta added that "Sister Bertha would really love to have you come up here again, so when you come back to America you had better save more than one week for Blowing Rock."

Moses Cone's obituary appears at length in the December 12, 1908, issue of the *Textile Manufacturers Journal*. It recounts the facts of his death as follows:

Moses H. Cone, president of the Cone Export and Commission Co. New York, one of the best-known men in the cotton goods manufacturing world, died at the Johns Hopkins Hospital in Baltimore, Md. on Tuesday. . . . The immediate cause of his death was heart trouble.

After a detailed account of Moses Cone's business career, the obituary continued:

In 1895 four thousand acres were purchased at Greensboro as a site for the Proximity Mills. The

White Oak Mills were erected several years later. These mills turn out the largest denim production in the world, for domestic and export consumption. Mr. Cone took an intense interest in fruit culture, having a very extensive fruit farm at Blowing Rock, in the mountains of North Carolina. It was here where he had expressed a wish to be buried that his remains were carried after the funeral in Baltimore. . . . He is survived by a widow. His death will make no change in the selling corporation, of which his brother Ceasar Cone is the head.

Brother Moses left half of his considerable estate to his widow and the remainder to his seven brothers and three sisters. They reacted in varying ways to the loss of their family leader. When strangers were shown through the Cone mills they would be informed by the brothers that such and such an arrangement was the way "Brother Moses would have wanted it." Bertha and Etta stayed on at Moses' home, Flat Top Manor; neither woman could bear to leave the ground where Moses was buried. Dr. Claribel went off to Europe for the summer, taking Bertha's sister as companion.

After the death of her brother Etta continued to correspond often with Gertrude, but she had nothing to report except her terrible, aching grief and her doubtful will to live. Too, Etta no longer felt the same about confiding in Gertrude. It was no longer Gertrude, now it was Gertrude and Alice. Although both the ladies at 27 Rue de Fleurus delighted in Claribel, Alice Toklas and

Etta Cone never went beyond the polite formalities. Miss Toklas found Gertrude's old friend from Baltimore hopelessly bourgeois, stubborn, and opinionated, without really having any ideas of her own.

Gertrude Stein saved practically every letter that was ever written to her. Among more than a hundred letters she had received and saved from Etta was an undated note written on the stationery of the Hotel des Saints Pères. It reads: "To the friend who has been one of the real inspirations in my life with the deepest love and devoted friendship of Etta Cone." As time passed, the character of the correspondence between the old friends had altered completely. Now Etta and Gertrude wrote with an informality devoid of intimacy.

It was a prim, inhibited, maiden-ladyish Etta who stayed on at her brother's home. She taught the little children at her dead brother's estate and wrote scolding letters to Sister Claribel, who, Etta felt, was wasting her time with "flatterers" in Europe.

What Etta was not willing to acknowledge was that Claribel loved to be flattered, loved to be the center of attention, adored making dramatic entrances and exits. She was as theatrical as anyone can be offstage in broad daylight and still not be ridiculous. She was saved by her wit, a satirical sense of humor, and her lovely voice. Swathed in her Kashmir shawls, a silver skewer holding her bun in place, and decked out in her Hindu jewelry, Claribel brought it off—she had style. Those great appreciaters of style, Gertrude and Alice, thought Claribel grand. With them, she could do no wrong. So while Etta went to the sewing bees and birthday parties of the estate workers' children at Blowing Rock, Claribel was having a grand time in Italy and Paris and Germany, where she always enjoyed the pageant at Oberammergau and the Wagner festival at Bayreuth. When Claribel arrived in Florence, she got in touch with Gertrude, who replied:

> May 28, 1909
> Fiesole
> Friday

My dear Claribel

Hullo, there are not any cars just now but hope there will be soon. I won't be in town before Tuesday. If you would care to take a carriage up and walk home, come to lunch any day, you or you and your friend. Any way you like. There is another friend of ours now at Assunta's, a fellow by the name of Sterne. I am not sure but that you have met him. I am anxious to see you.

> Yours,
> Gertrude.

Signorina Gertrude Stein
Villa Ricci
Via Giuseppe Verdi 25
Fiesole
My dear Gertrude:

Thank you very much. We shall be so pleased to come to you for lunch 1 o'clock on Monday.

> Sincerely,
> Claribel Cone

These notes were, of course, written on the ladies' calling cards. Both Gertrude and Claribel used their calling cards extensively. Henri Matisse always used a calling card too. It was not merely a small elegance but a matter of necessity in making appointments and sending messages. There was no telephone at the Villa Ricci, or for that matter at 27 Rue de Fleurus.

Even at such a leisurely pace of life, somehow things did "get done." *Three Lives* had finally been printed in 1909 by a publisher in New York, the Grafton Press. Gertrude had borne the cost of publication herself. Reviews had been scattered and not overly perceptive.

Sally Stein was getting things done too. A partisan of Matisse, Sally was thrilled in 1908 when she helped organize a painting class in Paris where she and a small number of German and American admirers could work under the master. Unfortunately the students felt that imitation was the best form of flattery. Temperament and language difficulties, lack of a suitable space, and Matisse's annoyance at teaching imitators led to an early death of the school. It did not kill Sarah Stein's enthusiasm for Matisse. She and Michael continued to collect his work heavily. Through Sarah and Michael, the Cone sisters had continued their friendship and their intermittent purchases of Matisses. As Gertrude Stein said, there was a camp of Matisseites and a camp of Picassoites. Gertrude certainly considered herself generalissimo of the Picassoites; Sally no doubt saw herself as queen bee of the Matisseites. For all that, social pleasantries were social pleasantries and everybody continued to see everybody no matter which camp their artistic tastes placed them in. There were always defectors, chief among them Leo Stein, who had announced himself as through with modern art. Leo was in love with an artist's model named Nina Auzias, and Gertrude was offended by such unconventional behavior on his part.

By the summer of 1912 Etta had regained her spirits sufficiently to undertake a trip to Europe. She went with Claribel to Frankfurt, where Claribel was planning to work again at the Senckenberg Institute. Once more Europe worked its charm on Etta; she relaxed somewhat and began to enjoy herself. Early in September she wrote to Mike and Sally, "Here in Frankfurt my friends are doing all sorts of nice little German stunts to make me feel how glad they are to see me again and it has really stirred me up and I am delighted."

Once settled in Paris, the sisters went again to Saturday nights at Rue de Fleurus. It was exciting to Etta to see the new additions to the collection and to watch Gertrude dominate the scene as quietly and surely as ever. The one discordant note was Leo. He no longer explained the paintings. He was either moodily silent or absent from the gatherings. It was now Alice Toklas' job to talk to wives, initiates, and those wanting a guided tour of the studio.

Gertrude had a surprise for the sisters that autumn. She had been writing "portraits" of everyone she knew, starting with Alice Toklas, then Matisse, Picasso, other sculptors and painters and her New England friend Mildred Aldrich. Gertrude had written a portrait of Etta and Claribel, titled "Two Women." Claribel read some of it aloud. It began:

"There are often two of them, both women. There were two of them, two women. There were two of them, both women. There were two of them. They were both women. There were two women and they were sisters. They both went on living. They were very often together then when they were living. They were very often not together when they were living. One was the elder and one was the younger."

And on and on it went for pages, scrawled in Gertrude's almost childish handwriting in her French school children's notebooks.

Gertrude also showed them new work from her summer in Spain. Claribel was enchanted with the new pieces, and although admitting she had no idea what they meant, she read some of them aloud too, with great effect:

"Please be please be get, please get wet, wet naturally, naturally in weather. Could it be fire more firier. Could it be so in ate struck. Could it be gold up, gold up stringing, in it while while which is hanging, hanging in din gling dingling in pinning, not so. Not so dots large dressed dots, big sizes, less laced, less laced diamonds, diamonds white, diamonds bright, diamonds in the in the light, diamonds light diamonds door diamonds hanging to be four, two four, all before, this bean, lessly, all most, a best, willow, vest, a green guest, guest go go go go go go go. Go go. Not guessed. Go go. Toasted susie is my ice-cream."

Gertrude called the piece "Preciosilla." She was delighted with the way Claribel had read it.

That summer the sister also went to visit Matisse at Clamart, Issy-les-Moulineaux, a suburb of Paris. Here his wife had a flower garden, he a huge studio, the children more space to play. For all that, Matisse soon missed Paris. He continued faithfully his habit of drawing from the model, so he had an excuse to go to Paris each afternoon to sketch. The Cone sisters, Michael and Sarah, and the Matisses would sit near the colorful flower garden, which included American wild flowers Matisse enjoyed, and sip tea while Matisse told anecdotes in a delightful manner.

When the sisters returned to Baltimore after the summer they got on each other's nerves even more than usual. At the heart of the problem was Claribel's lack of stimulation in Baltimore. After the end of the school year of 1909–10, it had been announced that the Women's Medical College of Baltimore was to close its doors forever. The small, lightly endowed institution could not meet the standards set by the American Medical Association. Thus ended Claribel's twenty-year career as a medical teacher and administrator. Her association with the research laboratory at Johns Hopkins had lessened when her great favorites, Dr. Osler and Dr. Welch, were no longer there.

Still, she hoped that somehow she could organize her research, which dealt primarily with the behavior of fatty tissues in normal and pathological conditions, so that it could be published. This remained only a dream. Each year when she sailed for Europe, Claribel would leave four or five hundred pages of an unedited, incomplete manuscript with her brother Sydney, who was also a doctor; if her ship went down, he was to try to arrange publication for her work.

In Claribel's desk were boxes and boxes of letters she had saved over the years. One was from Dr. Welch, head of the Hopkins Pathology Department. He had written Claribel years earlier: "For your own good, conscientious scientific work I entertain the highest opinion, and it has always been a source of satisfaction to me that you have worked so faithfully in my laboratory, where in many ways, including the work of instruction you have been of much assistance. For all this I thank you very heartily." Perhaps Claribel saved the letter because she sensed that it was as close as she would ever come to success in her medical career.

Although Claribel had given up all of her former Baltimore activities, she still accepted occasional engagements as an after-dinner speaker. Her underlying feelings about that period in her life crept into a talk entitled "Your Health," which she gave to a women's group at this time:

"Madame President and Ladies of the Council: Bernard Shaw says, the tragedy of modern life is that nothing happens, and the resultant dullness does not kill."

Etta now had her own small apartment at the Marlborough. She hung her *Yellow Pottery from Provence,* set out her few Matisse bronzes of the artist's children. Her Japanese prints and Picasso drawings were in port-folios, handy to show any interested visitor. Her grand piano was covered with a gorgeously embroidered Indian shawl. Although she did not own such monumental paintings as her Paris friends, Etta's apartment, and Claribel's as well, had much in common with 27 Rue de Fleurus and 58 Rue Madame. The sisters' special passion for exotic fabrics gave the rooms a richness uniquely their own. It was apparent that both responded to color: to crimsons, vermilions, cerulean blues, sharp yellows. A passionate pleasure in color made it easier to appre-ciate what Henri Matisse was trying to do. The sisters were able to enjoy paintings through an avenue of ap-proach that would have been less accessible to them if Matisse had not used a brilliant palette. They had lost interest in the work of Picasso for that reason, as well as being put off by the harsh rigors of his cubist composi-tions.

It was a bad winter that year in Baltimore; a severe influenza epidemic swept the city. Etta came down with it and, bedridden, called friends until she found one who could recommend a nurse. Pretty young Nora Kaufman was selected. Although Etta was then forty-three and her nurse just twenty-five, the two women got along splen-didly. When Etta recovered from her illness she pro-posed that Nora accompany her to Europe in the summer of 1913. Etta had become more decided in her ways in recent years and was tired of catering to Claribel's de-mands. The two sisters wearied each other with quarrels when they traveled together. Gertrude Stein loved to tell of an occasion when Etta asked Claribel to put up with an inferior hotel for just one night. Claribel refused, replying that one night was as important as any other in her life and she must be comfortable. Picasso had saluted Claribel's grandeur by nicknaming her "The Empress."

Yet, because she did not like being alone, Etta had been reluctant to travel without Claribel. Now she had Nora Kaufman to oblige her, as she had for so long obliged her elder sister.

Etta wrote to Gertrude, informing her of plans for the forthcoming trip. The sisters and Miss Kaufman would all go to London first, separating on the Continent later. Etta also replied to comments Gertrude had made concerning characteristics Gertrude shared with Claribel: "Yes, you are right," Etta wrote, "that it is a toss up as to which, you or Sister Claribel, likes being lionized the most. She sure like it powerful well. . . ."

When the old friends were together in June having tea at 27 Rue de Fleurus, Gertrude and Alice met Nora Kaufman and decided she was fine. They discussed happenings in, of all places, New York City. Since Paris always seemed more immediate to the sisters than New York when they were home in the United States, New York news six months old could be relatively fresh to them. In February there had been an International Exposition of Modern Art at the Sixty-ninth Regiment Armory in New York. Matisse, Picasso, Braque, Cézanne, and others the Steins had collected were represented in the huge show of eleven hundred paintings. Gertrude's friend Mabel Dodge had been working with the directors of the show, Arthur Davies and Walt Kuhn. Mabel Dodge had taken every opportunity to point out to the intelligentsia in New York that her friend Gertrude Stein was trying to do in literature what Picasso and Braque had done in their cubist paintings. The newspapers said the exhibition had been inspired by "the degenerates of Paris," that the painters were fakers. One painting, *Nude Descending Staircase* by Marcel Duchamp, was the particular butt of jokes. Well, it was not so long ago that Frenchmen had scoffed at Matisse's *Femme au Chapeau* at the Autumn Salon of 1905. Now the painting hung in quiet dignity on the wall behind the ladies as they sipped their tea and ate the little tidbits Alice had prepared. Less than ten years had passed since the Autumn Salon of 1905.

When talk turned to the sisters' travel plans, Alice Toklas raved about the pleasant time she and Gertrude had had in Spain. She made out long lists of *pensions* and restaurants for the sisters, who decided to travel there together with Miss Kaufman. A week later Etta wrote from Burgos in Spain to thank Miss "Taklos" for her help. It could hardly have pleased Alice to have her name spelled incorrectly, but it was an error Etta made intermittently for many years.

Later in the summer the sisters parted, and while Etta and Miss Kaufman traveled, Claribel stayed in Florence, seeing a lot of Leo Stein. Claribel also shopped at Pedulla's her favorite shop in Florence for Italian art objects. Her collection of boxes—she had Florentine boxes, brocade boxes, carved wood and ivory, and many other varieties—was enlarged by a number of purchases that summer. Claribel loved boxes of all kinds and shapes. Her friend Gertrude loved to play with buttons, examining each with infinite care. Little interests like these they found relaxing.

Gertrude had also been through difficult times. She and Leo had finally parted—forever. The paintings and the furniture had been divided. Leo took the Renoirs and the Matisses; Gertrude kept the Picassos, among them the cubist paintings which so completely offended Leo's sensibilities. Leo had gone to live in Florence. He was still involved with Nina and with his health: his hearing was failing. What else occupied him, no one could discern. Gertrude and Alice set about replacing Leo's Italian Renaissance furniture with some really comfortable chintz-covered chairs and couches they ordered in London.

When Europe exploded with war in August 1914 Claribel was in Munich, Gertrude and Alice at Alfred North Whitehead's English country home. Etta had not felt up to Europe that summer. In the stampede that took place among Americans abroad, none of the three ladies bestirred themselves. After some weeks, accompanied by Mrs. Whitehead, Gertrude and Alice managed to get back to Paris. Mrs. Whitehead then proceeded to the front—to take her son a winter overcoat!

It must be said for both Claribel and her beloved Germany that her enthusiasm for the German people held steady through all of World War I. When Ceasar arranged for Claribel to return to America via Spain, with the American Embassy officials, she replied that that was simply out of the question, that she could not get ready to leave on such short notice and because of that would have to stay in Munich. Ceasar was dismayed but not surprised. Gertrude and Alice decided, after reading Etta's letter about Claribel's remaining, that her reason was that she could not submit to the rigorous physical examination at the German border. Claribel would not ride with two others in the back seat of an automobile and found it upsetting to be crowded that closely with her fellow men or women.

When she went to Munich in July 1914 she had planned a short stay. Now that she had taken up an indefinite residence there, a very serious money problem loomed. There was no way to get her own money from America. If her Rosengart relatives had not come to the rescue she might have been forced to go back to America. The Rosengarts lent her money and continued to do so all during the war.

One of Claribel's ways of dismissing details was to write lists for herself: "1. get red buttons. 2. write check for $1,000 to pay for antiques 9. tip room maid 50 cents." Usually Claribel's lists, which she called "The Day's Work," went on for two or three pages in her little notebooks. Making lists works well in exorcising ghosts; writing down the need relieves the writer of the obligation to carry out the deed. Having listed her good intentions at great length each day, Claribel proceeded to enjoy herself, succumbing often to the chance acquaintance, the unexpected. Her only correspondent during World War I was Etta. The two were more intimate when they were apart and wrote lengthily and affectionately. At elbow's length, little misunderstandings about how things should be done often would crop up. In September, 1915, Claribel wrote to Etta from Garmisch-Parten-kirchen:

"My dearest sister: I think very often of you and hope you are well. Take things a bit easy. That is the only way to make life worthwhile. I say this and have just finished writing for 3½ hours part of a long list of things I mean to do (or hope to do) this winter in München. My schedule of work if I finish ½ of all this I shall be satisfied. A man's reach should exceed his grasp else what's a Heaven for? Here it is wonderfully beautiful." Claribel never said exactly what work she was scheduling with such care.

The war years provided Claribel with sufficient isolation to bring her to more than usual introspection. She was learning about a most unusual person—herself. She wrote to Etta with a new insight.

"I am really very comfortable and very happy—only I am trying to think out some scheme of life in which I can find myself physically comfortable for upon that depends my capability for mental work—and that is necessary for me in Life. Yet I have come to realize that I am not a born thinker—over here they put me in the category of Poetry-Art. And when I say I have never written a line of poetry in my life, they say, not in that sense."

Claribel wrote Etta of a Hungarian poet who brought her his poetry to read. After the reading the poet said, "You gave just the emphasis, just the expression to the words and thoughts as I meant them." "He seemed to think that so curious," commented Claribel.

The necessity for expressing her attitude toward Germany and the Germans grew. In July 1915 she wrote Etta: "I am strictly neutral my dear sister," underlining each of the words. "Please do not mistake that," she continued, "but being in the midst of so much suffering, so much heroism and so much nobility of soul and self-sacrifice, I cannot but feel deeply sympathetic and sincerely interested in the cause of the German. This does not mean however that I cannot sympathize equally as much with all the tried peoples of the earth—who are suffering through this mistaken notion of upholding one's own dignity—I cannot lend my acceptance to a situation which makes it necessary for human beings to slay each other in order to make wrong right. But as all of the nations appear to be guilty of this error, I must complacently accept the situation and simply feel deeply for those poor maimed bodies and wounded souls that are the result of such a system of error. I speak of all the nations—for as Thomas Paine said years ago—'War is murder, all the more heinous for being gloried in. . . .'"

Late in 1916 Claribel abandoned her "bohemian apartment" in Munich, located over a shop, for a room at the first-class Regina Palast Hotel. Thus, Claribel had once more found that, much as she loved the arts and their creators, she was not conditioned to leading a bohemian life. She settled down to make herself comfortable in the middle of a country at war.

In December 1916, standing in the lobby of a concert hall in Munich, Claribel heard the royal family announced. The royal party proceeded to the stairs near her. "Along with the rest of the guests I bowed," Claribel wrote Etta. "The procession continued and I returned to the occupation of fastening the laces of my sleeve. My head being bent I did not see what was happening. Presently I was conscious of someone standing before me —and heard a voice say, '*Ich hatte Sie nicht gesehen.*' There stood the King—with outstretched hands—charming—apologizing for having failed to acknowledge my bow. . . ."

Etta lived quietly during World War I. Without Claribel, without her trips to Europe, life was a rather dull affair. She took Miss Kaufman to Blowing Rock to visit her family, she engaged in unexciting civic works in Baltimore, she played the piano, she wrote to Claribel —and waited.

When it was obvious that the United States would participate in the war, Claribel became uneasy. Her situation was no longer a particularly pleasant one, yet she had let time slip away from her, and now there was nothing she could do but stay on in Munich indefinitely. She continued to amuse herself; she was studying German. Her poets and her trips to auctions, where she bought antiques of all types, kept her pleasantly unperturbed until early in 1917. Then she received two letters written in February and March 1917, informing her that her elder brother Ceasar had died. It had taken two months for the letters to reach her. All of the letters Claribel had written since the beginning of 1917 had been returned to her. Roused from her lethargy, Claribel finally made inquires about getting home. Her letter home acknowledging Ceasar's death closes: "Be assured my dearest sister Etta that if traveling be dangerous I shall not come till later. So you need not worry about my safety. . . . The world is dark . . . very dark . . . for all of us, but it still has its bright spots—let us reach out for them."

From the middle of 1916 to September 1919, Claribel got no mail from the United States except the letters announcing Ceasar's death. When the war was over, letters from her family in America urged her to return immediately. Certainly Claribel then wished she could. Defeated Germany was not the happiest of residences; pleas for food and help came to her daily. Some she could and did help, but her resources were meager compared to the unhappiness and hunger and privation she saw every day among her acquaintances.

Yet even in the midst of so much distress the unexpected had a way of turning out well when it involved Claribel. For a few days after the war, local Bolshevists were in control of some portions of Munich. They took to searching the rooms of guests in hotels, looking, no doubt, for whatever could be eaten or sold. When the soldiers came into Claribel's room she told them she had nothing they would want, nothing illegal. They proceeded to search, and found in a Spanish chest of many compartments some bonbons Claribel had squirreled away and forgotten early in the war. They sat down in Claribel's room and divided the bonbons. After the last candy was gone they respectfully bowed themselves out of her room, no doubt as much taken by her charm as their monarch.

Claribel grew tired of the Germans; for the first time her letters spoke glowingly of America, of the "inelasticity of the German mind." Yes, Germany had order and culture and all that Claribel had for so long admired, but now she began to write nostalgically to Etta of buildings on the Johns Hopkins campus. She told Etta to give a donation in her name to the building fund drive for the Union Memorial Hospital in Baltimore. She asked Etta to send Christmas gifts to friends in America for her. Because of her prolonged stay in Germany, Claribel finally discovered she had considerable affection for America. The American "character" seemed more inviting to her than it had at any time in her adult life. She did not go as far as Gertrude Stein, whose favorite song was "The Trail of the Lonesome Pine," and whose favorite general was Ulysses S. Grant, but she looked forward eagerly to being in America again.

Arranging passage was no simple matter and Claribel complicated it by insisting she must have a stateroom for two. In the end, she held out long enough to get for herself a stateroom for three, which she found adequate.

Her possessions had again expanded hugely during her six-year stay in Munich and she despaired of ever getting them packed. She would decide to give some away, and then the next day she would decide that she would not. "I have among my possessions," she wrote Etta in 1919, "things I am almost willing to part with before coming home. It is hard however to part with things one has taken the pain, time and thought and trouble and pleasure to collect—and with which one has lived through times troublous and pleasant—and which therefore have gotten to possess a personal value—a sort of personified value—it is hard as you know for me to part with such things and yet I have almost brought myself to it . . . we shall see." Later in the same letter, speaking of Johns Hopkins, "I am intensely sorry McCoy hall has been destroyed by fire and the surrounding buildings—even that the university has been removed out to Homewood is not a joy to me—there again is my old habit of clinging to the old things—things as they were and tradition."

Etta wrote Claribel admonishing her not to let her many possessions keep her from an early return to America. Claribel replied, "You are right—do not let things consume you. But on the whole I find things so much more satisfactory than people. People are interesting but you cannot live with them as satisfactorily as with things—things are soothing, if they are works of art—most people are over stimulating—and nowadays the people who have suffered war and especially a lost war are irritating. Some are like a bitter medicine of which my last letter not sent says more."

In March 1920 Claribel's large flowing handwriting grew even wilder and she wrote Etta: "I am ready to take

119

myself out of Germany. But the things! the trunks! the boxes! the books! The people are hungry here—I would like you to send some packages if it is not too much effort."

In April 1920 Claribel wrote to thank Etta for her offer of hospitality in Etta's apartment, but declined fondly: "I cannot think of inflicting you with my idiosyncrasies. If I had money enough I believe I should take a room in a hotel and keep my apartment for 'office' purposes. . . . Surely a hotel, however is not a home—nor is an apartment—an apartment is a dwelling—not a home. I am sure you have made a home of yours dearest sister and I thank you most sincerely for inviting me to partake of it."

Just before she finally departed Munich in the spring of 1921, Claribel wrote Etta, "I shall be so glad to see you again my dearest sister and all my dear ones. A life time —many life times—wars, revolutions, upheavals, insurrections . . . strikes . . . strikes . . . strikes . . . all sorts of strikes and all sorts of changes have taken place since we have seen each other, and yet curiously enough I believe we shall both be just the same as before. That seems curious does it not?"

Four

The Marlborough

I T WAS NOT EASY to come back. Claribel worried
secretly about the reaction of Baltimoreans to her wartime residence in Germany. She loathed the thought of
trying to combine her newer purchases with the clutter
she had left behind in 1914.

Although she frequently professed love of family in
her letters, she dreaded the necessity of adapting herself
to the ways of others—something Etta would surely demand. Etta was still prompt, Claribel invariably late.
Etta would have her possessions orderly, Claribel kept
hers in piles. Their eight-year separation had accentuated all these differences.

Claribel's medical career was now ten years dead; she
knew she would never go back to the laboratory. Her

hair was gray, she had grown even heavier during the war, her clothing had become threadbare during the long years of isolation and needed replacing. She feared that she was penniless. While she was interned in Munich, rumors had circulated among the small American colony that the United States had confiscated the holdings of all citizens who stayed in Germany during the war.

Claribel's fears were groundless. She found on her return that she had become a rich woman. Since 1916 she had been credited with substantial dividends from her stock in the Proximity Manufacturing Company and the Cone Export and Commission Company. Her first obligation was to repay the Rosengarts; she paid her debt in dollars at a time when inflation had destroyed the value of German currency.

Next Claribel put into effect a plan, evolved in Munich, of setting up as a private museum her collections of paintings, fabrics, sculpture, antique furniture, her collection of boxes, prints, and jewelry. The apartment adjoining Etta's on the eighth floor of the Marlborough was chosen for the purpose—the two entry doors were side by side at the end of the public hallway. Etta's apartment was 8D, Claribel's museum occupied 8B. Each apartment had six small rooms, which seemed even smaller because of the magnitude and color of the furnishings and paintings the sisters possessed. When the sisters began entertaining again, there was barely room for the guests to pass each other, so cramped were their living rooms. Although the paintings were of necessity hung cheek by jowl, thus making it impossible to step back and look at an individual canvas, the overall effect was decidedly pleasant. The visitor physically felt color; the impact of the pictures was not only visual but sensual as well.

While establishing her museum and beginning the long arduous job of unpacking and arranging her collections, Claribel moved into a one-room apartment on the sixth floor of the building, which she planned to use only for sleeping and dressing. It was arranged that Etta would provide meals for Claribel and their youngest brother, Fred. Fred, the only Cone brother with an interest in art, occupied a small bachelor apartment on the eighth floor that connected with Etta's apartment. Usually Fred gained Etta's quarters by the doorway connecting the two apartments, trying to remember that Etta liked the door to be shut at all times. Claribel always rang Etta's front doorbell when she arrived; it was easier for her to do that than carry keys. Claribel and Fred paid for the meals they took with Etta, but were able to deduct the cost of a missed meal provided they gave Etta sufficient notice of their absence. Sharing costs did not settle the old problem of Claribel's dilatory ways. Whenever Etta scolded her sister for a late arrival, Claribel would say grandly, "If I'm not wanted here I'll eat elsewhere." She never carried out her threat.

By the time the Cone sisters arrived in Paris for the summer of 1922 and moved into their quarters at the Hotel Lutetia on the Boulevard Raspail at Rue des Sèvres, everything seemed to them to be as it had always been.

Michael and Sarah were living in a house on Rue de

la Tour; they welcomed the sisters into their circle again with genuine pleasure. It did not take the Steins long to realize that the Cone sisters had considerably more money than they had before the war. Michael and Sarah began urging Claribel and Etta to buy more important and expensive works of art than they had previously. No one in Paris yet thought of the Cones as collectors, despite their long friendship with the Steins, and Matisse, and despite all their purchasing of paintings and sculpture. Etta was known as a lady of musical and literary interests, Claribel as a scientist.

The sisters found Gertrude and Alice still living at 27 Rue de Fleurus. Gertrude Stein had changed. Although her books brought little financial reward, her growing fame and her painting collection put her in a position to hold court and give or refuse audiences as she chose. She found it helpful to have Alice Toklas available to "talk to wives" while she entertained herself with their admiring husbands.

Carl Van Vechten and Henry McBride were among her New York friends who were doing everything possible to further her career. In London, John Lane had published an English edition of *Three Lives*.

Ernest Hemingway was only one of many young American writers who were bringing Gertrude Stein their stories to read and criticize. Sherwood Anderson was an admirer of her work and a favorite at 27 Rue de Fleurus. A few of Gertrude's books were now in print. *Three Lives* had been published in 1909, *Tender Buttons* had been published by Claire Marie, New York, in 1914,

Geography and Plays was published in 1922 by the Four Seas Company, Boston, with a foreword by Sherwood Anderson. There now seemed a possibility that *The Making of Americans,* the lengthy book Gertrude had struggled with and finished long before World War I, might finally be published by an admiring young American writer, Robert McAlmon, who published under the imprimatur of Contact Editions.

At the tea table the sisters heard of Alice's and Gertrude's wartime relief work and their adventures with a Ford automobile nicknamed "Aunt Pauline," or "Auntie." Although she considered herself an excellent driver, Gertrude admitted she had trouble with the reverse gear. Her solution was simple: she always drove forward.

Gertrude told Claribel, too, of her reaction when she and Alice saw their first succulent sausage in a long time while in Mulhouse just after the war ended. Gertrude said to Alice, "Take care, it might be Claribel."

Gertrude was glad to see Claribel again, but both Gertrude and Alice continued to treat Etta as condescendingly as before.

The sisters learned that Pablo Picasso was leading a conspicuously different life. He had married Olga Koklova, a Russian ballerina, and they had a baby son, Paulo. Under Olga's tutelage, the reluctant Picasso was making an effort to enjoy the pleasures of success and money. He was not impressed with fashionable partying and celebrities, nor with Olga's formal dinner parties, but he sought to please her by trying to enjoy the activities.

Later Dr. Claribel saw an instance of Picasso's efforts to become an all-round family man. Nora Kaufman accompanied Claribel one day when Claribel went to sit for her portrait. The two ladies were taken on a tour of the house. In Paulo's nursery they were startled to see that Picasso had decorated the walls with conventional representations of nursery-rhyme characters.

After Picasso finished the ink portrait, Claribel decided to settle her account on the spot and raised her black, ankle-length skirt so she could reach the pocket in her petticoat where she carried her money. (Etta carried her money in the same fashion.) Claribel counted out a thousand francs in new bank notes and handed them to Picasso with thanks.

Whether it was the urging of the Steins, the sisters' new affluence, or the fact that Claribel was now the second oldest living Cone (Carrie was her senior), the Cone sisters finally began, in that summer of 1922, to buy expensive paintings.

It was then necessary to go to Bernheim-Jeune to buy Matisse's oils. There the sisters sat in comfort and leisurely examined dozens of paintings done by Matisse over a period of thirty years. The proprietors, Gaston Bernheim de Villers and Josse Bernheim-Jeune, who had had Matisse under contract since 1909, were always pleased to welcome the Cone sisters. (The dealers were brothers who used different names. They ceased representing Matisse in 1926.)

Although the sisters completely agreed that Matisse was their favorite painter, that did not relieve the strain of deciding which paintings to buy. They looked and then went away and talked; then they talked and looked some more.

Finally it was decided that Claribel would buy the powerful Byzantine portrait of a woman, *The White Turban*, which Matisse had painted in 1916. Claribel paid 8500 francs (about $500 at the rate of seventeen francs to the dollar) for *The White Turban*. Etta chose *Rest in the Country*, a gentle painting of two women sitting on a bench beneath soft green foliage, for 7000 francs. Together they chose an early Matisse painted in the 1890s called *The Invalid*, for 4000 francs. Another Matisse they bought was one of his numerous scenes of Etretat, a favorite site for painters; it cost 6000 francs.

Now that Matisse had settled permanently in Nice he rarely visited Paris. Whenever he came he saw Sarah and Michael and he also visited the Cones. His son and daughter, Pierre and Margot, were his trusted lieutenants in Paris; they often had tea with the Cones at the Lutetia and made trips to the framers whenever one of the sisters purchased a new Matisse. Margot occasionally designed frame moldings, so a number of Cone purchases had frames created by Matisse's daughter.

Through Michael Stein the sisters bought four Matisse bronzes of female nudes which Mike promised to ship to Baltimore. Through Sarah, Claribel let it be known to Gertrude that she would welcome the opportunity to purchase any paintings or antique furniture that Gertrude might consider selling. Gertrude could not afford to buy a new painting unless she sold one.

After three months in Europe, it was pleasant to return to Baltimore and await the arrival of the purchases. Michael Stein, who served happily as the Cones' informal agent and also as their Parisian banker, arranged all the bothersome details of shipping and packing, and made out the declaration forms for them. In November 1922 he wrote: "My dear Etta: There are seven cases in all. 1-2-3-4 are Claribel's, 5-6-7 are yours. They are now at Havre. My *expéditeur* found that there were boats direct to Baltimore and as that avoided the expense as well as the risk of train shipment from New York, they will be sent that way. I had at first made out the paper of declaration 'Purchased in various antique shops in Paris during the summer of 1922.' That would not do so I made out names as near as I could remember."

Mike Stein jotted on Etta Cone's declaration form for the American Consulate General the following:

14 paintings by Favre	2 engravings by Picasso
4 bronzes by Matisse	22 engravings by Matisse
1 etching Renoir	1 painting by Vallotton
1 painting Picasso	2 paintings by Sarah Stein
	1 drawing by Picasso

In a blank space left below the statement declaring all the itemized works to be original, Michael Stein wrote: "I further declare that it is impracticable to obtain declarations from the artists as they are either dead or their whereabouts are unknown to me."

If Michael Stein could use such a shortcut it must be assumed that the staff at the American Consulate in 1922 was oblivious to the Paris art world.

So the winter was slowly used to put the new treasures into place in Claribel's museum and Etta's apartment. Although the ladies were kept busy, Etta found time to practice the piano each day. Claribel attended all the concerts at the Lyric Theater. Her striking appearance did not go unnoticed when she floated down the center aisle to place herself in one of the first rows. Her large leather purse and sundries she placed on a second reserved seat next to her. Hundreds who did not know her by name knew her by sight. Even when Etta joined her, everyone watched Claribel.

Every Wednesday at eleven o'clock Etta's old friend Cecilia Gaul came to play four-handed piano compositions with her for two hours. Then she enjoyed one of Etta's excellent lunches featuring her favorite dishes. According to legend, Miss Gaul was the last American to study with Liszt, and after his death continued her studies with Anton Rubinstein. A brilliant career was predicted for her, as well as for her brother and sister, both talented singers. Money troubles forced her to return to America without her European fiancé, and soon a terrible fear of performing in public seized her. She had completed a number of successful European tours as a soloist but never played before an American audience. She met Etta, another pianist who never played in the presence of strangers, at the Peabody Institute.

One day, during the period when Etta's art collection was beginning to grow quickly, Miss Gaul became very upset and made an unusual number of errors at the keyboard. When asked at lunch what the trouble was, Miss Gaul explained that a Degas bronze of a ballet girl, which

Etta had placed on the piano, was disturbing her. The subtle asymmetry of the figure, balanced on one leg, so distracted Miss Gaul that she couldn't concentrate on the music. Etta nodded but said nothing. She remembered one social gathering at which a guest, crossing Etta's small living room, brushed against the piano, eliciting some unorganized sounds from it. Miss Gaul had hurried to the piano and resolved the accidental chord.

When the pianist returned for the following week's session she saw Etta's solution. Etta would not move the statue; instead she had her seamstress run up a tea-cozy sort of covering that slipped over the bronze. Miss Cone assured her friend she would not remove the cover until their meeting was over.

Although Claribel ceased all professional medical activities before World War I, she kept up her association with an organization of doctors called the Women's Medical Society of Maryland. Once a year Claribel entertained the group, in Etta's apartment, since Claribel's museum had long since claimed the kitchen area for a small office with a few paintings hung in it. (The bathroom was also used for extra hanging space, the bathtub proving an excellent built-in storage bin.) Etta was glad to have the doctors; she was admirably equipped for entertaining, as she had trained her cook well. Her small dining room, with the Matisse beach scene at Etretat behind the table, the silver service on the sideboard, the shield-back Hepplewhite chairs, the bouquets of brightly colored flowers, often crimson and violet anemones, standing in French brass milk jugs: all bespoke Etta's love of a well-kept, firmly ordered household. For state occasions Etta would lay her silver and china on a precious old altar cloth; for simpler festivities she chose from a huge store of linen and lace she had bought over the years in bazaars and shops from Venice to Canton.

One of the new guests that year was Dr. George Boas and his wife Simone. Dr. Boas had come to Johns Hopkins University in 1921 to join the Philosophy Department. Simone was a sculptress. They heard of the Cone sisters and their art collection from the sisters' cousin, Mrs. Ella Ulman, who then took Dr. Boas to visit. He showed such knowing appreciation of the art that the sisters began to invite him regularly to dinner. Their parties were necessarily small as there was only room at table for eight.

Through Dr. Boas the sisters heard of the first stirrings of interest in modern art in Baltimore. Some of the students at the conservative Maryland Institute, the important art academy of Baltimore, came back from a year in Paris, where they had gone to paint on grants and fellowships, full of new ideas. The Armory Show of 1913, almost ten years earlier, had gone unnoticed in Baltimore. Dr. Boas told the sisters he felt that Baltimore must make way for the twentieth century in art, that Baltimore modernists must be allowed to show their work, that art as taught at the Maryland Institute was impossibly old-fashioned.

When in the spring of 1923 they sailed to Europe, Etta had in her trunk a package for Michael Stein. He had written asking her to get him something not available in Paris or London—rolls for his new player piano. Etta had been glad to take the trouble for her "Mikey," a favorite all through the years.

Settled once more in the Lutetia, the sisters saw their friends, began their rounds of the antique shops, and settled down to looking at and discussing Matisse paintings at Bernheim-Jeune. Gradually Claribel found a new life in the 1920s which suited her even better than that of the cloistered laboratory researcher. In her new role as a "collector," she was much more involved than the uninitiated would suspect. She had so many things to attend to. She had to visit her favorite antique shops to bargain with dealers over Persian bowls or Indian shawls that were vital to her collection. Whenever she was in Paris she went constantly to art galleries, artists' studios, bookshops. She spent a few hours almost every day examining artifacts in the Louvre's Museum of Decorative Arts. She felt many of her own examples were of finer quality than those she saw in the museum. Then, if Etta were traveling, Claribel had to write lengthy reports telling of all this in detail.

Because Claribel had unusual attitudes toward her personal effects, they too took a great deal of her time. She had to go to the Bon Marché over and over again to attend to the myriad questions that accrued when one ordered dozens of pairs of silk stockings and dozens of handkerchiefs and wanted them not only monogrammed but numbered. Numbering her stockings and handkerchiefs made it possible to use them in strict rotation, thus insuring even wear. Trips to her dressmaker took up time as well. When there were fittings, Claribel wore two extra blouses under the new dress, to make sure the final fit would be roomy and comfortable. It was a tribute to her perfect aplomb that she was able to accomplish all this though barely speaking French. It did not hurt her dignity to insist that the manager in each establishment be summoned posthaste; if the manager did not speak English, he ought to! A wise manager would sense immediately that the lack was *his* and not Dr. Cone's.

Nora Kaufman once said of Claribel, "She could tear up a piece of paper, but she could not throw it away," and, "She loved to buy." In a different way than Etta, Claribel bought passionately and by the dozens. Ties for men were a big item. Here her system occasionally backfired when she mistakenly gave one of her brothers or nephews the same kind she had given him the year before. She bought Liberty scarves by the dozens, usually having ten or twelve dozen in her hotel room on approval. She would choose at leisure, then call for a messenger to carry away the rejects. Once she admired a sweater Miss Kaufman was wearing, and when Miss Kaufman volunteered to buy her one like it, Claribel answered, "No, get me a dozen."

It was indicative of the singular life the sisters led that during their residency at the Lutetia in the 1920s many well-known writers frequented the hotel, but the sisters knew none of them even though all had met Gertrude Stein or knew of her.

When William Carlos Williams came to Paris with his

wife Floss in 1924, Robert McAlmon made a reservation for them at the hotel. James Joyce, Ernest Hemingway, and others of the literary world passed some time at the Lutetia, yet the Cone sisters were oblivious to all of the modern innovators in writing—except their old Baltimore friend, Gertrude Stein.

Those who frequented Sylvia Beach's "Shakespeare and Company" bookshop similarly did not exist for the sisters: Nancy Cunard, H.D., Robert McAlmon's English wife Bryher, Djuna Barnes, Ezra Pound, Harold Loeb, George Antheil. They continued to move in a sphere of their own, shedding a warm, mellow, restrained glow that hardly reflected the wild spirit of the left bank of Paris in the 1920s. The "lost generation" was truly lost on the Cone sisters. Only a chosen few of the modern artists, painters, or writers came alive for the sisters, and fortunately their instinct has proved extremely accurate.

Although Claribel went to Europe each summer with Etta after World War I, she no longer could organize herself for the rigors of travel on the Continent, so the procedure changed from that of their earlier trips together. Etta would now see Claribel settled into the Hotel Lutetia and then, after a month or so, would leave Paris with Nora Kaufman or with another nurse-companion from Baltimore, May Nice. Etta's travels were as ambitious as ever; she went to numerous cities in Italy, returning again and again to see her favorite paintings and buildings, which were old and loved friends by now. Members of her family in Baltimore or Greensboro would intermittently make the Grand Tour, and would be grateful for seeing the sights with Etta, feeling that they were "getting more out of it." They were, but Etta wasn't always, since it took a great deal of energy to act as a guide for novice travelers. She was a large woman and she continued to be visited with intestinal complaints such as she had known in her younger days in Munich. Even something like a toothache could ruin a trip for her.

With Claribel based in Paris and Etta traveling, the two resumed a daily correspondence. Claribel's letters were lengthy affairs, sometimes twenty or twenty-five pages; often she was unable to get one of her letters into an envelope—so she would divide the letter in two envelopes and mark them envelopes A and B, so they could be read in proper sequence. It was something of a problem for Claribel to keep Etta's itinerary firmly in her mind, so that Etta would find a letter awaiting her when she arrived at a new hotel.

Etta wrote as faithfully, reporting on her travels, on the museums she had seen, on the objects she had purchased and how much they cost. How much everything cost was a matter freely discussed in the mail between the two sisters—Claribel thought nothing of mentioning how much her breakfast melon had cost her—and Etta returned the intimacy by reporting how much a favorite *pension* which they had stayed at since 1903 had dared to ask her in 1923! Bargaining with dealers was fun too —and it was fully discussed down to the last sou in the sisters' letters.

Each provided a certainty of affection and intimacy for

the other. By no means had their personality balance changed—Claribel still tended to be the talker she had always delighted in being. Etta was still shy with strangers. Claribel more than ever had to have life ordered to her comforts—though sleeping sitting in a chair, or fully clothed across her bed, which was a favorite habit of hers, might not seem a "comfort" to others.

Etta, too, had special comforts on which she had become dependent. A cheerful, intelligent paid companion who accommodated her was by now a necessity. The most successful one was Nora Kaufman, with whom Etta had developed a warm, firm friendship. Little private jokes between them accounted for the signature "Q.T.," short for "Cutie," which Etta always used as a signature in her notes to Nora Kaufman. Etta called her companion "Mac," and although Miss Kaufman always referred to the sisters as Dr. and Miss Cone in public, she addressed her employer as "Cutie" in letters. No one else enjoyed such a playful relationship with the seemingly austere Etta.

Sometimes Claribel's letters to Etta were prefaced with explanations to help key up the pages that followed, as was this one, written during July of 1923 from the Hotel Lutetia to Etta at the Hotel Royal Danieli on the Grand Canal in Venice.

"My dearest Sister—this is the introductory page to a letter written last night (36 pages—12 sheets) and then this morning another seven sheets—up to page 19 inclusive with the 2 introductory sheets—21 sheets in all—I am acknowledging your 11th communication which

came this A.M. (not 12th as I said somewhere) written in
Venice Friday July 27 on arriving—the one also written
the same day from Milan as you were leaving—came Saturday evening July 28. And the one written Wed. July
25 after you had just arrived in Milan came Saturday
morning July 28, such are the foibles of the mail. I am
always glad to get your letters and they interest me because they tell of you and what *you* are doing. One or two
have come almost every day. I am sending this long letter in three compartments—in envelope A sheets 1–15,
in envelope B, sheets 16–22. Mike Stein will be here soon.
Allan had the doctor puncture his ear drum to relieve
fluid on Saturday. With some relief—to his parents as
well, Love to you and to Cousin Julia. C."

Part of page 5, envelope A, included the following advice to Etta: "While you are in Italy you ought to be able
to get a cobbler's table to suit you—if you pay enough for
it—and if I were you and you see what you like, get it—
even if it is dear. —Make fewer presents to other people
next year and you can afford this luxury for yourself.
Here I am at the end of my sheets."

Page 6, Part B, continues: "On looking about I find
more paper—what I wish to say is this   Gertrude offered
so courteously and sincerely to bring me home from
Sally's in their machine on Friday night July 27 that I
said 'Yes.' We came at 10:30 P.M. I sat in Alice's place—
and she sat on the dashboard (?)——On the way home
Gertrude said with a little hum-and-haw hesitation but
prettily—'Claribel—I have a little table and a Stipo'—
I think she said—'that I am thinking of disposing of—

and I wondered whether you would be interested in it! It is in the dining room and I need the space for a larger piece of furniture for serving purposes.'

" 'Oh yes' I said, 'I am very much interested.' 'Then' —she said 'Alice would it be indelicate of me to ask Claribel to come home with us now to see it.'

" 'Oh' I said, 'I can see it another time—do not disturb yourself.'

" 'Oh' she replied—'I did not know whether it was indelicate of me to broach the subject so suddenly.'

"I assured her that I appreciate her 'indelicacy' as it will probably help me to get something I sincerely desire —However we went to 27 Rue de Fleurus and I saw the table and 'stipo' (I may have gotten the name wrong—) (later—I had) and took some soft drinks and talked things over.

"The table proved to be a light-colored Spanish? cobbler's table—very small—with a drawer. But Alice assures me as does Gertrude that it is walnut and that all it needs is rubbing with brush and wax etc. to make it as dark as their refectory table in their living room. In fact I think they say they (Alice) will do it. . . .

" 'I shall take it gladly' I said—and—'the rest'—— 'Perhaps you would rather let Mike decide the rest.'

"So there it is. Tomorrow if Mike comes at 2 30 P.M. as per engagement 'if nothing interferes' (he will) I shall tell him I have bought two small objects of furniture of Gertrude (I did over phone) please to fix the price and pay for them (He will) Gertrude in showing them to me said she had not the place for them—she needed that space in the dining room—and indeed she needs the money as well she said (to buy the other piece with) I told her whenever she has other pieces of furniture she wishes to dispose of not to hesitate to be 'Indelicate' again—I shall always be glad to get what she has—One never knows. . . . Gertrude's taste is subject to change—as is her taste in other things—and I—I hang on forever! Italy and Italian things are good enough for me! I find however—that people who live in France long get to have a liking for what they call 'good French things'—Gertrude and Miss T. busied themselves to make me interested in French things. Gertrude even went so far as to move out from the wall—a little Louis XV commode with really lovely lines and harmonious composition a 'signed piece' —which they discovered in a little place 'down in the south of France.' And pointed to the variety in detail of her French Credenza—etc. Then—they brought me home in their machine—'You like it here' Gertrude said as we got into the machine—'Very much' I replied— 'And do you still like the Germans better than the French'! (proselytizing!)——

" 'They are all human beings to me'—I replied whereupon she laughed with— 'which means that you do not care much for either of them!' whereupon I laughed —and she is neither here nor there for my meaning. Upon reaching home I invited them for lunch next Wednesday. 'That suits us perfectly' said Gertrude—'but you come to lunch with us—do come! It will be so nice!'

With that I agreed—said good night—and she rode off benignly—Goodnight and love to you my dearst sister—and to Julia. C."

While Etta traveled, she continually satisfied her long-time passion for buying beautiful lace. On her earliest trips to Europe she bought inexpensive pieces in the open-air bazaars in Italy; these were smaller versions of the flea markets in Paris where one could buy old as well as new things of all sorts. As her taste developed and her purse increased to support it, she bought more expensive items. Habitually Etta denied herself certain pieces she wanted as just "too expensive." This attitude occasionally backfired. The story goes that when one of her brothers brought his prospective fiancée to Paris Etta felt that she wanted to buy her a gift in honor of the betrothal. She took the girl to the Bon Marché, steered the young woman to the lace department, and invited her to pick any piece she liked as a gift. With the unerring eye of the novice, the girl picked a very expensive piece that Etta had been coveting for herself but had felt she couldn't afford. Etta was silent. Later, very perplexed, Etta went to her brother for advice. He said, "Of course you must buy it." So Etta did, and presented it to the innocent young woman, who subsequently did not marry into the Cone family. Years and years later Etta, still coveting the piece of lace, went to the woman, who by then had married another man and raised a family. Etta offered to buy back the piece at twice the amount she had once paid the Bon Marché for it as a gift. "No," said the woman, "I've grown fond of it over the years and could not part with it now at any price!"

Lace collecting had other frustrations. One year Etta bought one sleeve of a magnificent priest's surplice while she was in Italy. It pained her not to have the other sleeve, and her dealer told her the name of the man in England who owned the other half. They corresponded, but neither would sell, although both offered generous amounts to acquire the half they were missing. The offers went begging, and both collectors settled down to wait for the other to die, hoping no doubt that the coveted sleeve might then be bought from the rival's estate.

It was such forays into the world of laces and textiles, as well as return visits to favorite museums, that kept Etta busy and happy while traveling without her sister.

A list of some of Dr. Claribel's transactions while in Paris during the summer of 1923 hints at the shopping she busied herself with.

Lithographs of Bonnard, Derain, Renoir	645 francs
4 Favre paintings	1,000 francs
Milan lace & ring	80 francs
Spanish chair	412 francs
Handkerchief	120 francs
3 Matisse lithos	900 francs
lace	80 francs
3 chairs, box & brass (Raspail)	800 francs
shawls (Iranitska)	465 francs

Armoire & curtains 1,000 francs
Gertrude Stein (for furniture & paintings) 4,600 francs
carpenter work repairing an Italian chair
    and a Spanish chair 520 francs
framer 525 francs

The list continues with a payment to Matisse of 14,000 francs, the purchase of lithographs of Braque and Vlaminck for 405 francs; the next item listed is a payment to a carpenter to repair a sacristy table from Spain for 750 francs. There were expenses for cartons (22 francs), a tip for the packers of 40 francs, an electrician's bill of 85 francs.

Contradictory as such a list may seem, the sisters intuitively sensed the historical continuity in their collecting. Although early critics of Matisse, Picasso, and Cézanne suggested that these men were destroyers of the great traditions of French art, time has shown otherwise. The sisters' blending of the laces, furniture, brasses, and fabrics of sixteenth- to eighteenth-century France, Italy, and Spain with so-called "modern art" now seems valid. In the Parisian world the Cone sisters knew (the apartment of Gertrude Stein and Leo Stein, later Gertrude and Alice Toklas, the homes of the Michael Steins) these seeming contradictions melted under the authority with which the Steins put together their surroundings. Yet the Cones did not imitate the Steins—they couldn't have, because the Steins never agreed among themselves for long and were constantly changing their minds. Gertrude came to be glad to be rid of her Matisses, Leo abandoned his Picassos to Gertrude once cubism came along, the Michael Steins sold an early great collection of Matisses only to found another Matisse collection. Leo later sold a superb collection of Renoirs to buy Coubine—who he claimed was *the* artist of the twentieth century. After World War I Gertrude took up with a French painter named Favre who was at best an imitator of Matisse. Gertrude thought for a brief while that perhaps Favre was to be *the* artist.

The Cone sisters bought more than their share of Coubines and Favres, and later went on to make their own mistakes. What the four Steins offered their friends was an American-born, socially acceptable *ambiance* in Europe. One friend had said of Michael Stein, "He liked doing business but he did not want to be *in* business." Since his early days of taking care of the financial affairs of Leo and Gertrude, Michael was used to the pleasant busyness of suggesting, guiding, assisting. The Cone sisters were grateful recipients of his willingness to do this for them, year after year. The Cones availed themselves of all four of the Steins in much the same way one can use the facilities of the British Museum. The Steins were there for the Cones and many other Americans—to stimulate, to inform, to assist, to introduce. In Europe, the Steins were their milieu, in Baltimore their collection was their own. And it was now growing very quickly, in both size and stature.

By the end of June 1923 the sisters had made up their minds which Matisses they would buy for the year. Having at last grown accustomed to choosing and paying for important paintings, they bought at Bernheim-Jeune with a much more lavish hand than the year before. On June 21, Bernheim-Jeune entered in their ledgers the sale of six Matisse paintings to the Cone sisters. Of the six paintings bought that day, five averaged around 12,000 francs, or about $700; the highest price they paid was 17,250 francs, about $1000 for *Still Life with Dahlias*. The other paintings included:

10,250 francs—*Odalisque with Tambourine*
9,500 francs—*Girl at the Window, Sunset*
12,000 francs—*The Music Lesson*
12,500 francs—*Woman with Violin*
12,000 francs—*Still Life*

Thus fortified, Etta set out on her annual pilgrimage to Italy. Two weeks later Claribel decided she could not do without two other Matisses they had originally rejected, so on July 6 she went and bought another painting showing the beach at Etretat and *Girl in a Green Dress*. Each of these paintings cost more than $700, or 12,500 francs. The sisters had come some distance from plucking Picasso's drawings off his studio floor and paying a pittance for the artist's work.

One day that summer of 1923, Claribel happened to walk past Berlitz in Paris. She decided to go in and arrange to have a trial French lesson. If she liked it, she planned to continue three times a week with private lessons. Claribel liked the trial lesson and scheduled the first class. Its postponement because of other unexpected pressing matters turns up as a recurring theme all through Claribel's marathon letters to Etta that summer. Claribel finally remarked, "You have heard the lesson mentioned so often, you will probably expect me to talk French when you return." Claribel could not talk very much French, but that did not usually concern her, since she preferred to let Etta do the work of ordering meals and instructing cab drivers. Etta's French remained simple, flat, unaccented, and adequate.

Claribel frequently wrote Etta detailed accounts of her visits with Gertrude and Alice. She had brought Gertrude a gift, some monogrammed handkerchiefs, which excited both Gertrude and Alice. Claribel wrote, "Gertrude is full of appreciation of the wonderful handkerchiefs I gave her. They are the most beautiful I have ever seen and she and Miss Toklas say so too. She said she was at the linen place on the Rue de la Paix & while waiting for Alice she looked over their monograms and found nothing to approach her monogram. It is the most beautiful G.S. she had ever had or seen. And Alice brought out their best G.S. embroidery from Spain which she thought wonderful until she saw mine. Gertrude had hers (the green one) sticking in her sleeve (Green Java Dutch print) she showed to me—'You may be sure I do not blow my nose on it,' she said, 'they are not for everyday use, such handkerchiefs as these'—and 'Alice washed them herself for fear they may not last long enough'—and then Alice ran all over the house to get other linen to show how much better these are than anything they have. Their appreciation was so childlike and touching

—I suggested that if I find no monogram to suit me as well I shall have G.S. put on mine whereupon G. laughed like a child with 'that would be quite dangerous.' Well that's the way we spent our day. The food was good—duck and zucchini, etc."

Claribel had always been a great walker, and she continued her habit: "I walked to Place de la Concorde intending to walk all the way home—but the park of Champs Elysees and Place de la Concorde looked so inviting that I sat on a bench in the shade and punctuated my 'Je prend Il prend Vous prend, etc.' for as you see I had my Berlitz with me and was studying French. I punctuated this with various forms of observation upon the couples of lovers who sauntered through or sat in the Park—and—it was all very interesting. Then I was very tired from the study not the punctuation so I let a cabman drive me to the Brasserie."

Then Claribel switched back to her other favorite topic, Gertrude Stein. "I got you a copy of *Vanity Fair* which included Gertrude in several lists of authors to 'avoid'—one list by Mencken. But as she is classed in one with Shakespeare, in another with Goethe, Jane Austen and the like it is a compliment. She continues to be visited and lionized by all sorts of 'interesting' people—people organizing social work—sculptors—women adopting 21 orphans, men gathering material for literary papers, Journals, etc.—all of which keeps her in a happy state of tension—and in the midst of it all she carries my embroidered monograms up her sleeve (not to blow her nose upon) and is happy. And Sally, in a tone of poking

fun at Gertrude says—'and a few days ago I went over to
Gertrude's to see your furniture—the first time I have
been there for a year'—and she said (imitating her, Gertrude, submissively) 'Sally would you mind taking these
books home one at a time and see which I ought to pub-
lish first?' Of course Sally felt mightily flattered—she
really looks up to Gertrude in a way—although she says
to me 'neither you nor I care a hang what Gertrude
thinks of us—if she is disagreeable it is all right and if she
is pleasant—it is just the same to us—and this keeps Gertrude guessing.' This is a funny world I say to Etta
Cone."

As Etta proceeded on her travels in August, Claribel's
lengthy letters continued to roll forth, dwelling now on
shopping sorties, now on the Steins or the Matisses. Occasionally Claribel grandly set her younger sister straight
for some minor misdemeanor: "What I started to say
around the margin of page 11 was—is it not a little indis-
creet to write the price of your rooms 35 fr. a day on a
post-card which can be read by every official and other
person in this hotel—especially when my mail has been
perambulating about indiscriminately as I wrote above.
It might make them less willing to reduce our rates. Of
course had you not been tired you would have waited to
record this in a letter."

Another letter might contain a compliment for Etta:
"Today, while with Gertrude, I happened to remark—
'Etta has a charming home—she has beautiful things'—
Gertrude said 'Well Etta is essentially a home-maker—
she had a charming home on Eutaw Place even before

she had so many beautiful things. Etta would have a nice home anyway.' "

Claribel's next letter might be condescending: "You need not hesitate to write me anything—I shall always be interested in what you have to say and think—and it may relieve you to express yourself. Your love of Venice and what its historic and cultural beauties mean to you is quite touching. Florence will say even more to you I am sure. . . . Please do not forget when you are in Florence to let Assunta box up my books (mostly art books—Berenson, Walter Pater, *Flame of Life*, etc.) and send them to me in Paris. I do not believe the other things I left there have much value. I forget.—Leo & Nina have not yet appeared in Paris—they are now with Nina's relatives up in France somewhere. I believe Leo's family do not look forward to his visit with a delightful anticipation." Leo and Nina had been married in 1921 and were living quietly outside Florence.

Claribel wrote Etta at some length of a visit she paid to Henri Matisse: "My dearest Sister: Mon. Matisse and Margot have just left—they took tea with me—of this more anon—Now a quick telling of my yesterday's visit with the Matisses. When we were leaving Margot drew me aside with—in French—'You remember when we visited you—you offered me the use of that lovely rose shawl of yours. Now may I make so bold as to ask you to let father use it for a picture? We shall be in town tomorrow. May I call for it?' 'Yes' I said. 'In the morning I have a French lesson—will you come in the afternoon?' 'At what time?' 'As you will.' 'Three P.M.,' she said. 'Yes,

come and take tea with me.' She said her father would be
with her—she would bring him along (not quite so in-
formally however) and they came and I lent her the shawl
—and she says her father will make a painting of her in
the black velvet she wore the evening they spent with us
—and that shawl and we all think it will be lovely. She
was interested to know what I thought of the pictures her
father brought back and which I preferred. He did only
4 large paintings 1 of which he will keep (the least important one) and 7 lovely lithographs. He wishes to show
that he is not considering himself or Bernheim-Jeune
first. Apropos of my remark to Sally as to our having
third or four choice, Sally says that is why he asked us out
—rather complimentary was it not?"

The following week Claribel visited Gertrude again
and amused herself and pleased Gertrude by reading
aloud one of Gertrude's new compositions. ". . . did I tell
you of going home with Gertrude and Alice and reading
aloud one of her latest called an 'Elucidation.' but does
it elucidate? 'However it is very pretty, isn't it!' Gertrude
said with satisfied amplitude. Amplitude is the word—
'Satisfied amplitude' is a good Gertrudism for something
she has written and sits in her chair listening to with
great satisfaction beaming from her face and her whole
ample form so she listened with 'satisfied amplitude'
—do not forget this expression and someday—if you remember it for me—I shall ask G. whether this is worthy
from her point of view—to take its place in the new literature. She quoted at length passages from Shakespeare
not nearly so clear as hers—(she said) It may be true. C.

"Now—I hope you will get to Florence—I know you love it—If you get there have a good time—and please remember me to our friends; and if not too much trouble please have my books sent to America or here as you think best."

Although Claribel was now much less of a recluse than she had been during World War I, her letters were frequently peppered with remarks on the joys of single existence: ". . . I just read over the letter I wrote last night and enjoyed it very much. What do you think of that? Well, whom are you to enjoy if you cannot enjoy yourself—and my mania for living alone has taught me at least to get some entertainment out of myself . . . tomorrow I shall take my first real Berlitz lesson in French. The 1st was a trial lesson."

And later in the same letter: ". . . I am glad you have two rooms in Venice—it will be more restful for both you and your companion. The constant being together is hard on people. . . . The best of friends I believe, need a rest cure. I think Mike and Sally see too much of each other; as do most husbands and wives. Love and write soon C."

When her patience with people gave out, then Claribel would give herself up almost entirely to what she found to be her deepest satisfaction: ". . . the days are not long enough for me even when I am alone. I enoy the study of things so much—and most people irritate me."

In this mood, Claribel would spend her mornings in the Louvre's Museum of Decorative Arts looking at furniture or textiles. In the afternoon she would make her usual rounds of the antique shops and buy.

At the end of the summer Claribel even grew weary of Etta, and threatened to write her only once a week to "save time." She also asked Etta to save all her letters and return them to her at a later date. Etta always saved her elder sister's letters, realizing that most likely hers had been thrown away. Although Claribel found it impossible to throw away old newspapers, she could be cruelly casual about her sister's letters.

When the sisters returned to Baltimore in the autumn of 1923 they busied themselves setting their new purchases in place and inviting favored friends such as Dr. Boas in to see the new Matisses. They heard from friends that the new Baltimore Museum of Art, which had opened in temporary quarters in the Garrett mansion on Mount Vernon Place, was progressing nicely, if not spectacularly. The museum had been formally opened on February 20, 1923, and its director, Miss Florence Levy, had high hopes for it. One of the first exhibits was a sculpture show of American artists. Outside, more statues were grouped around a reflecting pool in Mount Vernon Place. A group of enthusiasts was urging that Henri Crenier's bronze fountain figure *Boy and Turtle* be purchased by private subscription and given to the city. Miss Levy wrote of this project, "A number of contributions of $10 and $25 each have already been pledged to the Museum for this purpose and it is hoped that the Municipal Art Society will help."

Although the sisters were happy to help the new museum, it did not occur to anyone to ask for a loan of any of the paintings they owned. In 1923, the museum did not want them. There were circles in Baltimore that regarded the Cone sisters as eccentric if not slightly crazed to collect the paintings they did. Dr. Boas had been "warned" about them by an earnest lady friend before he began to visit them. Miss Kaufman bravely repeated to the sisters some of the stories she heard about them. She knew from past experience that their reaction was to laugh. The sisters had also been the butt of family jokes for years. Their brothers thought Claribel and Etta were throwing good money away. Since it was the sisters' own money, what could anybody say? The brothers were nonetheless gallant enough to advance funds for painting purchases when the ladies became momentarily overextended.

How can paintings that look insanely ugly and perhaps crazy become just ten years later not only completely acceptable but highly fashionable? Gertrude Stein understood public switches from hating to revering paintings and painters. What had happened simply was that time had passed. Something that had once looked dreadfully new and shocking had become a classic. She wrote:

For a very long time everybody refuses and then almost without a pause almost everybody accepts. In the history of the refused in the arts and literature the rapidity of the change is always startling. . . . When the acceptance comes, by that acceptance the thing created becomes a classic. It is a natural phenomena a rather extraordinary natural phenomena that a thing accepted becomes a classic. And what is the character-

istic quality of a classic. The characteristic quality of a
classic is that it is beautiful. Now of course it is perfectly true that a more or less first rate work of art is
beautiful but the trouble is that when that first rate
work of art becomes a classic because it is accepted the
only thing that is important from then on to the majority of the acceptors the enormous majority, the most
intelligent majority of the acceptors is that it is so
wonderfully beautiful. Of course it is wonderfully
beautiful, only when it is still a thing irritating annoying stimulating then all quality of beauty is denied
to it.

It was not only their collection that might have given
rise to small stories about the Cones. They were so individual in appearance that no community, other than one
as cosmopolitan as Paris, would have let the sisters slip
by unnoticed. Claribel liked to be noticed; and she took
little trouble to hide or change the activities that were
sure to increase the stories about her. Her many colorful
shawls worn one atop the other, the silver skewer stuck
in her hair, were familiar to many in Baltimore. On the
eve of one of her departures for the train to New York to
sail for Europe, Claribel stayed up all night packing.
When morning came, she still had not finished. Her bed
was strewn with her unpacked handbags—ten or twelve
of them. Unable to decide which to take, she resolved the
problem by dumping them all into a string bag which
she carried on her arm to New York.
On another occasion while Claribel was in Baltimore

she became ill with the flu. After Dr. Osler died she would never let any other doctor tend her but she did not mind having Nora Kaufman help her. So Claribel called Nora and asked her to stop by her apartment on the sixth floor of the Marlborough. When Miss Kaufman arrived she found Dr. Claribel sitting up in bed with three thermometers in her mouth. Laughing, Nora Kaufman waited until she took them out, then questioned her on the need for such a procedure. Dr. Claribel answered, "I haven't used them for a long time, and I wanted to make sure they were accurate."

Because Dr. Claribel was always behind in the execution of her elaborate plans she sometimes got a whole year off schedule. On one occasion she brought home a trunk from Europe, half filled with linens she had bought abroad. When it came time to pack the following spring, she had not emptied the trunk. She sent it back to Europe and returned with it the following autumn, now completely filled with linens. Her tardiness in unpacking became a problem only when the United States customs men wanted her to pay duty again on last year's linen which had made three ocean voyages untouched. It took a great deal of scrambling before Dr. Claribel produced the right papers and proved half the linens were not dutiable.

So the good doctor added to the little legends about her that existed in Baltimore. By the 1920s, a new generation of academic and medical people wondered—if they thought about it all—what had become of Women's Medical College and whatever had happened to Dr.

Claribel's medical career. Many in Baltimore called her
the doctor who had "never practiced." Her medical activities before World War I were almost totally unknown. It was also generally believed that Dr. Claribel
had gone to medical school with Gertrude Stein—who
had begun to interest some students at Johns Hopkins.
All the facts had been slightly muddled or forgotten and
Claribel was not particularly interested in correcting the
record. She was too busy having a wonderful time with
each day and its possibilities. Priding herself on being
"up" on civic life, she would save yesterday's newspaper
to look at tomorrow. Because of her inability to throw
things away, yesterday's newspapers, like the porridge of
the "Sorcerer's Apprentice," would occasionally threaten
to engulf her one-room apartment on the sixth floor at
the Marlborough.

As 1923 closed, letters containing romantic news from
Paris headquarters arrived at the Marlborough. Mike
Stein wrote to Etta about the wedding of Matisse's daugh-
ter Margot to George Duthuit, an art historian.

"Dear Etta: We have been in a whirl of excitement.
Firstly the Matisse wedding. We sent for you and Clari-
bell a mahogany Louis XVI round table which turns up
on hinges. Gabrielle, Sally and I were the only people at
the luncheon at Lapérouse's except the family and the
witnesses. The couple have gone to Vienna and Matisse
back to Nice to his work. There are some new lithos
which I have ordered for you. . . . Allan and Yvonne will
be married in February. . . ."

Allan Stein, the curly-haired little boy of Picasso's drawing and Etta's first years in Paris, had grown up and was about to marry Yvonne Daunt, a young dancer in the Paris Opéra ballet. Allan, a willful and moody young man, had been something of a problem to his parents; and the problem had not eased as the years passed.

Gabrielle Osorio, a well-educated Frenchwoman who had once been married to a prominent French politician, had come to live with Mike and Sally. Gabrielle and Sally were both Christian Scientists. Madame Osorio had adopted a young girl, Jacqueline, who became a favorite of the Stein household. After Mike completed his letter to Etta, Sally and Gabrielle read over the account of the Matisse wedding and found it lacking in important details. The next day Gabrielle wrote to Etta, setting the record straight.

"Dear Etta: . . . Yesterday, Mike read us his letter to you and I felt that you would be interested to have more complete details about Mlle. Matisse's wedding—details which of course a man could not think of giving. The marriage took place at the mairie of the 6th arrondissement on Place St. Sulpice. A motor car was sent for us at 11. There were quite a number of people, music & flowers although the ceremony itself was very short and simple. Her witness was the painter Marquet. . . . Monsieur Matisse seemed very much moved. The bridegroom looked very handsome and so radiantly happy and the bride was lovely in a white taffeta dress with ruffles embroidered with silver and gold. The bodice (or waist as you say in America) was tight-fitting, short jacket, closely

buttoned down the front and also embroidered. On her
head was draped an Egyptian scarf, spangled with gold,
loosely drooping over one shoulder and held up behind
with a gold comb—the young couple have gone to
Vienna for their wedding tour. . . ."

By June of 1924 the sisters were back at the Lutetia.
No sooner had they settled down comfortably than Etta
received a letter from Gertrude Stein. It read:

22 June 1924

My dear Etta

I want to tell you something a propos of the thing
you mentioned in connection with the autographed
Three Lives selling for $13. It seems that the latest
passion of the art collectors in America is the buying
of manuscripts ever since Quinn made such a success
with Conrad and *Ulysses* manuscripts. . . . Some one
has suggested my selling the manuscript of *Three Lives*
for a thousand dollars, I don't suppose that you want
to pay any such price for a manuscript but since you
had a connection with that manuscript I want to tell
you about it before I consider doing anything. I think
it's kind of foolish but I wouldn't want you to think
that I would sell it to any one else without telling you
about it first,

à bientôt
Gertrude

Considering that Etta had once given her free time in
Paris to type the book for Gertrude, the request must

159

have seemed singular to Etta. Yet, because she was unable to show her anger directly to Gertrude, she sent off this mild reply:

Monday June 23, 1924

My dear Gertrude:

I do indeed appreciate your kind thought of me in realizing my personal pride and interest in your *Three Lives*.

I simply have to face the truth and that is, that I am seriously considering putting all I can spare of what I have left of my income in a Renoir painting. This, with other expenses somewhat heavier than usual are handicapping me a bit this year.

Elsie and Adele as well as we have engagements for Tuesday evening and regret extremely that we cannot come to you. Perhaps one day next week or the latter part of this.

Yours as always
Etta

In the years that followed many heard of Gertrude's request and Etta's refusal. All who knew of it heard about it from Etta Cone, who nursed a sense of hurt toward Gertrude for the rest of her life. Possibly the hurt was a more cumulative one than Etta cared to acknowledge.

Etta began that year to take abroad with her young friends and relatives to give them a taste of continental travel, as well as to have them serve as her junior companions. The young ladies mentioned in the letter to Gertrude were the daughters of Ida Gutman, who had

Claribel Cone as an intern at
Blockley Hospital, Philadelphia,
c. 1888.

Etta Cone as a young woman
in Baltimore.

Johns Hopkins graduating class, 1901. Gertrude Stein on balcony, third from right.

Getrude Stein, monumental in a bird bath, early 1900's.

Assisi, 1903: Etta and Claribel Cone.

Florence, the same year: Claribel, Gertrude Stein, Etta.

Front porch of Cone home about 1905: back row, Julius, Sol, Clarence, Fred; front row, Moses, Bernard, Sydney, Ceasar; the boys, Herman, Sydney, Jr., Benjamin.

India, 1907: Bertha, Etta, Moses, and Claribel on elephant.

The famous Stein studio, 27 rue de Fleurus, Paris.

Michael and Sarah Stein's studio, 58 rue Madame, Paris.

Studio occupied in 1905 by Picasso, rue Ravignan, Montmartre.

Paris: Dr. Claribel, Miss Etta, Daniel Stein (son of Allan, grandson of Michael and Sarah), Michael Stein, Mme. Osario.

Portrait of Leo Stein by Picasso

Michael and Sarah Stein in Paris.

ta Cone with "friends," Perugia.

Dr. Cone in her robe, Florence.

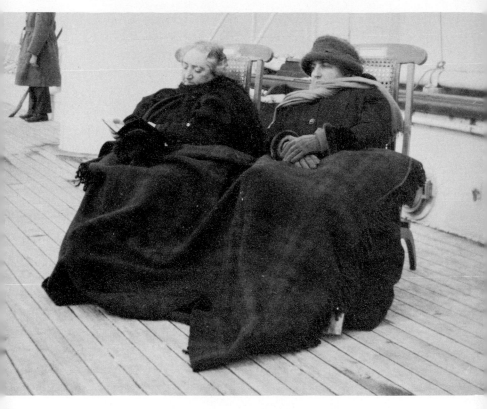

The Cone sisters (Claribel, left) on the *Statendam's* deck, 1928.

Claribel at Lac Léman, Switzerland, 1929.

Etta Cone, shortly before her
death, in Baltimore, 1949.

Front sitting room, Claribel Cone's Baltimore apartment, with Van Gogh *Shoes,* Matisse paintings and sculpture.

Claribel's "artistic" bathroom.

Corner of Claribel's back sitting room, with Rodin bust, Cezanne *Mont Ste. Victoire.*

The front sitting room; sculpture and oil by Matisse, Picasso mask over arch.

Opposite, above:
Hall in Claribel's
apartment, with Matisse
Serf, Nice, sari lampshade
and brocade door covering.

Opposite, below:
Etta Cone's dining room.
Cézanne *Bathers* on left,
three Matisse oils over
back sideboard.

This page, above:
Picasso *Mother and Child,*
antique fabrics on couch
and cushions in Etta's
sitting room.

This page, below:
The same room, with
Picasso *Le Coiffure,* two
Degas bronzes, Picasso
Monkey and *Woman with
Bangs,* and Renaissance
chests.

This page, above:
Etta Cone's main sitting
room. Manet pastel over
mantel, left of Gauguin oil

This page, below:
Etta Cone's hallway stored
huge amounts of fabrics,
objets d'art, lace—and
priceless modern art.

Opposite, above:
Etta Cone's back sitting
room, with Zorach head
of Etta, Renoir
Washerwomen, and early
Picasso circus watercolor.

Opposite, below:
L. to r., Etta, Claribel,
Gertrude Stein, two
preliminary Matisse
sketches of Etta, Matisse
sketch and photograph.

The Cone wing of the Baltimore Museum of Art.

been Etta's dearest confidante in Baltimore many years before. Dr. Claribel was much less enthusiastic about introducing the young to the beauties of Europe. She had instead employed her college-age nephew Sydney, Jr., to serve as her secretary in Baltimore. Sydney came every Sunday morning and worked for four hours at an hourly wage of a dollar and a quarter. He found it difficult to make any real dent in Claribel's affairs since she insisted that he record each bookkeeping entry in quadruplicate.

Nora Kaufman was also with Etta that summer of 1924. Altogether she made nine trips to Europe with Etta between 1913 and 1929. She got to know and enjoy all of Etta's favorite painters, churches, and museums. She watched her employer glow over Matisse's *Interior, Flowers and Parrots,* one of Etta's favorites. Miss Cone's companion knew how much she loved her Renoir, *The Washerwoman,* how much she was moved by her classical Picasso, *Mother and Child.* Always it was Dr. Claribel who bought and enjoyed the sterner stuff, such as Matisse's early bronze of *The Serf* and Van Gogh's oil of *Shoes.*

So off went Miss Cone and Miss Kaufman on their annual travels. The young ladies stayed behind in Paris but Hortense Guggenheimer's son, Richard Moses, traveled with Etta. Hortense, wife of Judge Jacob Moses, had died in the flu epidemic of 1918. Her son Richard had been living abroad since his middle teen years and could boast a wide set of acquaintances among the artists of Paris. Gertrude Stein had once, when he was a child, asked him to call her "Auntie Gertrude."

Claribel's usual barrage of letters followed the travelers. She wrote Etta of a series of Shaw plays she was attending with Mike and Sally in Paris. They had seen *Man and Superman* and *Pygmalion,* and had enjoyed them. After admonishing Etta not to give herself so freely to her friends, Claribel closed her letter: "It will not hurt you if you leave a little of the over-consideration for others (except me) aside. They will probably just let you alone—but that is a small matter. They will want you the more. This is a dissertation on the egoists of modern life —but I must be off—Take care of yourself and have a good time. Being free-lancers there is nothing in the world for you and me to do but have a good time in our own way—and there is nothing in the world for us to be —but be happy—This is my will and testament. Love to you and regards to Miss Kaufman. Affectionately, Your Sister Claribel."

Claribel had an unusually distressing summer. She had lost a purse containing a $500 letter of credit and 60,-000 francs. When Claribel lost anything she was always afraid to tell Etta. After a while she would, knowing that a scolding would follow. While Etta was away from Paris traveling, their bank representative called on Claribel to get information about the lost letter of credit. Claribel wrote of this interview: "He was very charming of course, and to prove to you that he was not disconcerted at my attitude to this incident he spent over an hour with me. Oh my! How I wished it was you talking to him—and I eating my much longed for breakfast! But no he stayed and stayed. (Is it possible he wanted a tip?) Shameful thought, I am surprised at you, I hear you saying. Then why did he stay? And I was so hungry! Was it to practice his English—and to let me practice my French? Deliver me from bucolic conversations in foreign tongue."

Some five pages later Claribel completed her letter to Etta with "I have been making the rounds of our Antique, Persian, Oriental shops. All are very charming (they are French!) and all ask for you—I am beginning the buying all over again—but shall stop—How these Aboyas wrap themselves about me! How the Saris wind themselves about my very heart. 'Throat' would be better for they strangle out all other impulses—and the metal bowls and the jewels. Now that I stop to reason about it, it is silly foolishness, this collecting of things! But it must have some solid foundation—some foundation deep in the hearts of people—for look at the thousands who are moved by the same impulse—and look at the Museums that have been founded to satisfy this impulse. It is the craving for beauty that is such a vital function of the human soul—that's it—the craving for beauty—for perfection—some say that it is one way of finding the path to God—is it?"

Before the summer was out, Claribel's losses also included a package of antique textiles she had taken on approval from one of her dealers. It was a week before she could bear to mail the letter she had written to Etta immediately after her loss. Speaking of the lost fabrics, she wrote, "I am just as composed about this loss as though the things were at home in a trunk—but Oh they were so beautiful! The curious thing in the psychology of all these losses is that they do not hinder me from continuing my nefarious practices—only death will do that I fear—or a reversion to my original profession—the microbes —and that is an idea is it not? I must be off—and I cannot blame you for button-holing me. I am buttonholing myself. But I am rejoicing in discarding another bad pen. I look about me and here in the writing room is a stub pen. How little it takes to make me rejoice these days. Just as little as it takes on the other hand to annoy me. Life is made up of little messes, as well as the big things."

Claribel's museum was a going concern by the winter of 1924–25. She wrote long lists in her notebooks of those who had come and those she had promised to invite. The younger painters in Baltimore were eager for invitations. They had heard of the wonders of the museum from Dr. Boas. One young lady who came at Dr. Claribel's invitation unwittingly became the cause of open warfare between the conservatives and the modernists in Baltimore art circles. Miss Shelby Shackleford was a promising student at the Maryland Institute who had won a scholarship to paint abroad for a year. The scholarship provided for an exhibition of her year's work at the Institute. The director of the Institute, Hans Schuler, was horrified by the modernity of the paintings Miss Shackleford brought home and forbade the exhibit. What followed was, for Baltimore, a major explosion.

The December 11, 1925, issue of the *Sun* stated that another modernist had offered Miss Shackleford exhibition space. Miss Irene Susanne Gogel, a piano teacher,

offered the use of her studio. Miss Shackleford accepted
the invitation and the exhibit opened on December 19.
Two days later the *Sun* headlined: "Modernist Artists
Plan Association."

The local art critic was having his troubles too. The
Sun had as art critic in 1925 a quiet, slender young man,
A. D. Emmart, who, aware of the atmosphere of hostility,
would "slip in" an occasional favorable reference to the
merits of some of the modern art he knew and admired.
Each time, such praise would bring a delegation of ladies
and gentlemen to the offices of Emmart's superior urging
that Emmart be fired. For better or worse, Baltimore was
now decidedly aware of modern art and artists.

Etta had continued to correspond with Gertrude in
spite of her private sense of grievance. Gertrude wrote
that winter: "My dear Etta: That was awfully nice of you
to send $100 to the Mildred Aldrich fund. We are trying
to save her home for her and it looks as if we might do it.
Anyway thanks. You will be pleased will you be pleased
that two sisters are being printed in a book along with a
lot of other authors, will send you a notice by and by
also Making of Americans starts to print all of which is
a pleasure, well anyway happy New Year to you and Claribel and thanks. Gertrude."

Mildred Aldrich was a writer who had been loyal to
Gertrude for many years. She had lived in a house near
the Marne during the World War I battle, and had written a book about her experiences there. She received
other help from Gertrude and Alice, who decided she

should have the *Légion d'honneur* and pulled strings until she did indeed receive the award. Mildred Aldrich had always stoutly believed in Gertrude and waited for the day when the *Atlantic Monthly* would accept her.

"Two Sisters" was Gertrude's profile of Etta and Claribel. She published it under the title of "Two Women," calling Etta "Ada" and Claribel "Martha," in Robert McAlmon's *Contact Collection of Modern Writers*.

Claribel found when she got to Paris in 1925 that it was becoming easier and easier to bring herself to buy expensive paintings. At the end of June she cabled Cone Export in New York, "Bought pictures. Cable me through American Express, Paris, twenty-thousand dollars in Dollars. Claribel Cone, Hotel Lutetia." She then noted the wording of the cable and its cost, eighty-six francs, in her little notebook and went off again to look long at her newest acquisition. It was a late Cézanne of the artist's favorite scene, *Mont Ste. Victoire*. Claribel had bought it from Bernheim-Jeune for 410,000 francs. It cost her about $18,000—much more than she or Etta had ever paid for anything in their collections. Before Claribel picked it up on July 1, she used to go occasionally to the Louvre to examine the Cézannes through opera glasses.

Claribel really enjoyed her buying that summer. She bought some choice items from Gertrude, with Mike serving as intermediary. One was Marie Laurencin's first painting of herself, Guillaume Apollinaire, Picasso, and Fernande Olivier, for which she paid $500. The painting is known as *Group of Artists*. Marie Laurencin had given the painting to Gertrude Stein and was furious with her when she learned Gertrude had sold it. Claribel also bought Picasso's *Head of Man* of 1905, a masklike relief, for which she paid Gertrude $200. And she bought a new Matisse, the *Oliviers*, paying Pierre Matisse $1500 for his father. Etta bought a more expensive Matisse, *Interior, Flowers and Parrots*, which cost more than twice as much as Claribel's. Etta could afford to, as she had not bought herself a Cézanne. Now she might buy one, though; once Claribel owned a different painter's work, Etta had an overwhelming urge to own his work too.

One of the hazards of buying art is the possibility that the collector might mistake flattery for friendship or, worse still, for evidence of artistic talent. Etta enjoyed the company of lesser-known young painters who sometimes charmed her more by their attentions than by their work. She seemed untroubled by the possibility that one artist hoped to sell his work when he paid flattering attention to her. He wrote to inquire about her health, volunteered to squire her and her sister to exhibitions, and was willing to write a long essay on the meaning of his work. In the end, her instincts as to what was a good painting usually saved her from serious error.

Certainly the artists hoped—and Etta gave them every right to hope. She made great exceptions for artists. Artists could have mistresses and illegitimate children—not because this was the way one should behave, but merely because they had the artistic temperament—and well, that was that. All that Etta would never forgive in her

family or at home she gladly and happily forgave her artist friends. The young French artist Favre stretched
Etta's forgiveness too far. He was expected one afternoon
to squire Etta to a museum and made the error of keeping her waiting forty-five minutes. She bought only one
more Favre painting. Eventually she and Claribel tired
of his work and gave away as gifts all of his paintings.

Whether this tolerance of artists and their ways extended to Gertrude Stein seems doubtful. The sisters
never ceased to be fascinated by Gertrude—they never
openly broke with her, there was no reason to—but they
did not see much of her after the mid-1920s. Perhaps because they had known her in Baltimore the Cones regarded her somewhat less generously than Picasso or
Matisse. They knew Gertrude's Baltimore relatives, and
it was a little hard to swallow the notion that the friend
who had spent so much time with them in years past was
a real "lion" in Paris—with young writers and poets and
painters delighted to sit at her knee.

Though there was an observable cooling in this direction, friendship was still very lively among the Cone
sisters, Sally and Michael Stein, and Henri Matisse. Claribel, feeling gay the summer of 1925, decided to give a
dinner party for the Matisses in the Lutetia dining room.
She worked out a careful seating plan in her little notebook for the occasion. When the Matisses arrived
promptly at seven forty-five one evening in July, the
party went to the hotel restaurant. Etta sat at the head
of the table, with Madame Matisse on her right, Henri

Matisse on her left. At Claribel's end of the table, Pierre Matisse was on her left and George Duthuit, Matisse's son-in-law, on her right. They spoke English to Claribel. Sally Stein sat at Matisse's left hand, Mike across from her; a Cone cousin, Hetty Guggenheimer, and Margot Matisse completed the party. Thanks to her ability to converse with Matisse in French, Etta finally sat at the head of the table, Sister Claribel at the foot!

When the sisters ate alone or with lesser luminaries they ate at the Brasserie, a considerably cheaper restaurant in the Lutetia facing on Rue de Sèvres. Nephews, antique dealers, minor painters, and poets were frequent dinner guests. Some of the guests came repeatedly because it was a good chance to get a free meal.

Paris was so much fun that summer, Etta stayed on longer than usual. Mike and Sally were involved in a fascinating project with Madame Osorio. They were building a house designed by Le Corbusier. Located on the outskirts of Paris at Garches, the house was startling and modern. The architect felt he made a major concession when he finally allowed the Steins to bring their Renaissance furniture into his functional, clean-lined, plate-glass structure. The furniture and the brocades and the Matisse paintings fitted into the new house amazingly well. All agreed that the effect was stunning. Matisse was dazzled to see his paintings in the new surroundings.

When the house was completed in 1927 Etta and Claribel visited *Les Terrasses* a number of times, enjoying Sally's excitement and Mike's pleasure in having something new to put to rights. Mike had moved in his player piano and treated his guests to recitals by his favorite pianists. Sally served them homemade ice cream.

In Paris the Cone sisters often saw two young second cousins—Richard Moses and Richard Guggenheimer. The latter was from New York and the sisters had not met him until he came to Baltimore at the age of seventeen to study at Johns Hopkins. Now he was in Paris hoping to become a painter. Etta had interested herself in him and was helping him finance his art studies although his family wanted him to be a lawyer and not a painter.

The two young men had managed to strike up an acquaintance with Isadora Duncan, who was also living at the Lutetia. The boys conceived the notion of introducing Claribel and Etta to Isadora. The sisters were interested; they had always admired Isadora's art. The next problem the young men faced was who was to come to whom. Claribel and Etta were not used to waiting on other ladies, especially strangers. Neither was Isadora. The young men finally arranged matters so that one Richard was dining with the Cone sisters in the Brasserie when the other happened to pass escorting Isadora. Introductions were made, and it was decided they would all visit together after coffee. The Cone sisters invited Isadora up to their rooms, she asked them to come to hers. They won, perhaps by virtue of superior numbers. While the two young men enjoyed watching the results of their enterprise, Isadora told about her adventures at Bayreuth with Cosima Wagner. It was at Bayreuth that Claribel and Etta had first seen Isadora dance in 1903. Claribel told Isadora how much they admired her work and what she stood for. She thanked them with, "If more people understood as you do, I would have had my school long ago." When she finally got up to go, Claribel also rose. For a moment the two stood and stared at each other, then Isadora left. The sisters never saw her again.

Nice little things were always happening to Claribel; often, though they seemed unimportant, they left Etta choked with envy. When the sisters bought theater tickets in Paris they sometimes took Miss Kaufman and one of the Richards with them. Whichever Richard it was, he was also instructed to go to the theater and purchase tickets. Two of the seats had to be in the first row on the aisle. One was for Claribel, the other for her packages and purses. The others always sat ten or twelve rows farther back. The party went in that fashion to see a ballet premiere. After they were seated, Etta saw Picasso sitting alone across the aisle from the majestic Claribel. At the two intermissions Claribel and Picasso sat and chatted. Etta would have given anything not to be sitting twelve rows behind her sister that night.

It was in 1926 that the art world finally acknowledged the Cone sisters as collectors. Dealers in Paris all knew the two fat, rich ladies from Baltimore, dressed meticulously in ankle-length black dresses. They were always treated with the exquisite courtesy reserved for those who combine breeding with money. But it was men like Dr. Albert Barnes, Stephen Clark, the Russian Shchukin, and

John Quinn who were known among the dealers and painters as the big collectors of modern art, particularly of Matisse.

When John Quinn died he left his collection to his sister, who was made very nervous by such an unorthodox possession. The good lady from Ohio and Quinn's other executors agreed that they had better sell while they could, so auction sales were hastily arranged in Paris. A smaller sale was arranged in New York. Pierre Matisse, the artist's son, had opened an art gallery in New York. When Quinn's Matisses were to be offered for sale the executors of the estate checked with Matisse to see if he knew of any American collectors who were interested in particular paintings. Pierre made a trip to Baltimore to see Dr. Claribel and Miss Etta. He found the sisters nervous, indecisive, less than happy to be approached to buy a painting. People were always approaching them to buy laces, books, all sorts of objets d'art. Matisse thanked them for the tour of their apartments, where some of his father's most beautiful paintings hung, each frame hugging the next. Their collection was already so large that the sisters could no longer see the color of their walls—they were completely covered with paintings.

When the Quinn auction took place in Paris, Pierre Matisse was startled to discover himself bidding against Dr. Claribel for *The Blue Nude*. The situation demanded the ultimate courtesy, and Pierre dropped out of the bidding. He noted wryly to himself that Dr. Claribel finally bought the picture at a price higher than she could have bought it for through him in America. The very notoriety of *The Blue Nude* served to mark out even its third owner as an art collector of considerable daring. Although the painting was already twenty years old, although it had hung first in the Stein studio and then in John Quinn's home for a number of years, public revulsion against the painting was as strong in 1926 as it had been in 1907. It was considered the classic horror of that horror known as modern art. Most American collectors were reluctant to buy any nude in 1926, much less *The Blue Nude*. Dr. Claribel, her inner excitement tremendous, paid 101,000 francs for the painting. She could hardly wait to see the painting in her living room. She could hardly wait to show Baltimoreans that naked lady. Etta was somewhat dazed, but in her eyes the master could do no wrong. *The Blue Nude* was a classic, and that was that.

By now every dealer and curator in New York knew that the two ladies from Baltimore had an important collection of Matisses, some great Cézannes, some excellent Renoirs, and others of the big names. The Cones had arrived. New York museums and dealers wrote asking to borrow paintings for various loan exhibitions, but Claribel and Etta did not respond enthusiastically. Few collectors do. Collectors miss their paintings. The passion that causes them to go to considerable trouble and expense to collect demands that the paintings be where they belong: on their owner's wall.

Before it was time for Europe again in 1927, Etta spent a few weeks in New York. She naturally went to the art galleries. At Henry Reinhardt's gallery she saw a Van

189

Gogh flower painting that very much appealed to her. Uncertain whether to buy it, she wrote Claribel, who answered: "As to the Van Gogh, of course at this distance it is difficult for me to give my advice. If I were considering putting $4000 in a picture I should wish to see it several times before deciding to buy it. If it were for myself this is what I should say: Van Gogh is very great. He was one of the biggest influences on Cézanne and certainly on Matisse—and many of the later men. Everything that he has done is strong and virile (almost too virile sometimes) and his paintings are attractive. I wonder whether he will remain 'the fashion.' He seems a bit less in the limelight than he was some years ago—so much for his name—but for the particular picture you have in mind—of that I should say if it is pretty (which you say it is), attractive, and if it is decorative and pleases you—why care a darn what anybody else says of it. It is true $4000 is a big sum to put into a picture, but if you want a Van Gogh (is it signed?) and find this a good one—and if it gives you a thrill why I guess the thing for you to do is to take it. . . ."

About this time Claribel realized her health was beginning to fail but she discussed it with no one and continued to live as usual. She began each day as she always had: marking new pages in her interminable notebooks with eight categories of activities for the day ahead: 1. Miscellaneous 2. Work 3. Read 4. Evening 5. Remember 6. Letters 7. Visit 8. Miscellaneous. She and Etta entertained at dinner frequently. Then Claribel wore a deep red velvet gown trimmed with gold lace, completing the costume with a black Liberty scarf, amber beads, a silver dagger in her now silver hair.

The sisters decided that the answer to Claribel's health problems was to choose a new locale for Claribel while Etta traveled in Europe.

Their choice of Lausanne turned out successfully. Paul Vallotton, brother of the Swiss painter, Felix, had a gallery in Lausanne. Before long he was busy showing the sisters paintings and visiting them at their hotel for tea. Claribel bought Van Gogh's *Shoes* from him but worried as to whether it would look well in her museum. It was not particularly attractive, she wrote Etta, but after all, it was a Van Gogh. While Etta was off traveling, Claribel bought from Vallotton a bronze cat from dynastic Egypt. Something about this small ancient figurine thrilled her hugely. She had not had that same exquisite excitement since she had bought *The Blue Nude*. The cat pleased her differently. Its age, the mystery of its creator and his intentions, she pondered and wrote on all through the summer.

Claribel, still assuming that Etta was also in the habit of destroying letters she received, wrote again asking Etta to save Claribel's letters for their writer, since surely they had no further value for the recipient. Etta replied that she had always kept Claribel's letters, and surely their writer might see them again. For the first time in her life Claribel saved Etta's letters that summer, noting carefully on the envelope the hour she had received them and the hour when she had allowed herself the pleasure of reading them.

The Cone collection continued to grow. By early 1929 the sisters owned a few dozen Matisse oils and over a dozen bronzes, innumerable drawings by Etta's favorite artist, their fine collection of Picasso, their Renoirs and Van Goghs, as well as their large collections of fabrics and laces. Claribel found herself wondering what they would eventually do with all this. Etta could not bear to think of death or dying, but Claribel realized that it must be faced. She was ready to face it. She took a long look around her—at the city where she had grown up, where she had become a doctor and had done her research, where she had founded her own museum, where she had been the object of some attention and occasional ridicule. She thought of all the people she knew who laughed at her, at her collecting, and then she thought about the future. The future belonged not to her and not to those who had alternately ignored or ridiculed her. The future belonged to those who were making it. Certainly the paintings she owned were part of that future. Should she pay Baltimore back in kind and give the paintings to another museum, such as the Metropolitan in New York? Should she leave the collection to her family? They had not shown any particular interest in art—old or new. Although they had always been loyal, that did not guarantee that they would not sell the collection at auction after her death or Etta's. Claribel saw the answer. The one person she could trust was Etta. Etta knew, Etta loved, Etta cared. Yet that was not enough, because Etta was too much given to fastening on personalities and making outsized heroes of them. Claribel must set an ultimate and determining goal for Etta. What was the goal to be? Not to send the pictures to a posh, big-city museum in New York, not to allow the collection to be dispersed by the family or the executors as John Quinn's had been.

When Claribel wrote her will she found that the words came easily and succinctly. She who had drafted each speech for a women's club five times over finally knew what she had to say. The art collections were to be given in toto to Etta upon Claribel's death. Claribel said that they were to be given to Etta with the hope that, "if the spirit of appreciation of modern art in Baltimore should improve," Etta would subsequently will both collections jointly to the Baltimore Museum. The ultimate disposition of the collections was to be of Etta's choosing. If the spirit of appreciation in Baltimore did not improve, the Metropolitan Museum was Claribel's second choice. She also left $100,000 which would pass to the museum with the collections.

Pleased with her will, Claribel sailed with Etta and Miss Kaufman on the elegant new *Statendam* for their annual summer abroad. After Claribel was settled into the Lausanne Palace Hotel that summer, Etta and Miss Kaufman departed for Munich. Two days later Claribel wrote a letter to Etta. This one was never mailed. It read:

"My dear Sister Etta: Last night I had a pain in my heart—the first one I have ever had. This morning my pulse omitted a beat on several occasions—for that reason—and in view of the fact that I have reached the age at which the eldest members of our family die I am writing this letter to say good-bye to you my dearest sister who have always been so good to me (Also to my very dear Brothers, Sisters, nephews, nieces). When one begins to grow feeble one is a useless member of society—so I should say I go without regret—except for the momentary pang of regret (this blot is ink—not a tear although it should be that!) it may be to my dear Brothers and Sisters. Give my best love to all—to my brothers, sisters, nephews and nieces and grand-nephews. I should like you dear Etta to select from my things—or to buy for each of them something they may'like. Of course for you and the Collection I should wish the suitable things saved. . . . I expect to write again! You see I am only *one* of the many millions who have passed on. (will have passed on.)

"Say goodbye to Miss Kaufman for me. C.

"I love my family both in Greensboro & Baltimore very much although I am too lazy to express it."

Claribel addressed the letter to "Miss Etta Cone, Lausanne Palace Hotel," dated the envelope on the upper left-hand corner, then put it away in her room. Early in August Etta returned to Lausanne from her travels. Since the sisters were expecting their brother Fred to join them, it was decided that Miss Kaufman should return to the United States.

Claribel and Etta lived quietly in Lausanne, seeing their friends the Vallottons, or "business associates," as Claribel referred to them, looking at art, reading art books, shopping for linens and laces, taking walks around the town, taking an occasional excursion on Lake Leman. Claribel made no mention of her premonition of death. There was no need to. In September, soon after Fred's arrival, Claribel caught a slight cold that developed into pneumonia. Within a week she was dead.

Etta learned that she was going to have to go on living,

and alone. All that she had dreaded, that she had never even dared think of, had happened and she went right on living. And there were so many things to be done. She sent the necessary wires to Baltimore and Greensboro, and she acknowledged the black-banded cards and letters that flowed into her hotel room. And she sent for her Miss Kaufman and her Miss Nice. Her message to Miss Kaufman said: "Get Miss Nice as your companion; I will not be a very happy one." She knew that having them would not make her less alone, but it would be good to have them anyhow. So she and Fred stayed in Lausanne and waited for a direct train to bear Claribel's body to a Dutch port—to be placed aboard the *Statendam*. In death as in life, Claribel was to be comfortable. No local, meandering train was to be entrusted with carrying her toward the boat on which she would have traveled home if she could have chosen. The mantle of the dead sister had come to rest on the living sister. None of Claribel's clothing was to be destroyed or given away—it was to be folded in tissue and returned to the Marlborough, as were her papers and books.

After arrangements were made, Etta returned briefly to the Lutetia with her brother to settle Claribel's affairs before returning to Baltimore. Among the many letters of condolence Etta received, a few meant a great deal to her. The widow of Moses, Sister Bertha, who had gone around the world with Claribel and Etta twenty years earlier, who had danced with them at galas of the Sociables forty years earlier, who had drawn comfort from Etta's presence at Blowing Rock after the death of Moses, wrote to Etta early in October:

"My dearest Etta: It is a relief to see your handwriting —and for you to write that you are fairly well is a great comfort to me—I cannot tell you ever how greatly shaken I was and upset when Herman called to tell me the awful news from Europe—Every night since I have seen Claribel at her best—with so much knowledge and information and such enjoyment in what she did, and wanting to go on, it does seem terribly unfair, when so many others are tired and ready to go—nature is fearful and wonderful. . . ."

Another letter read:

October 16, 1929

Miss Cone
Hotel Lutetia
Paris France
Dear Miss Cone:

I know the words lose all meaning in the presence of great emotion but allow me to communicate of my painful shock in learning by a letter from my family of your sorrow. I am thinking of your immense grief, knowing as I do of your attachment to Dr. Cone and being able to guess how much her rich and distinguished personality could have added to your enjoyment of life.

Do believe, dear Miss Cone, that I share your grief profoundly.

Affectionately and devotedly,
Henri Matisse

1 Place Charles Felix
Nice

Etta replied: "Dear M. Matisse, Your letter full of appreciative understanding of my sister's character touched me deeply. Allow me to express myself frankly in saying that knowing you and your great work was one of the great influences of her life as well as my own."

And there was an exchange of letters with Gertrude Stein.

> Bilignin
> par Belley
> Aix

My very dear Etta:

I have just had word from Mike of the death of Claribel and it has saddened me terribly, I was awfully attached to her, oddly enough just the other day we were telling that delightful story of Claribel and the box in her room with the two old bon bons and the Bolsheviks in Munich, everything she did had an extraordinary quality all her own, I had not seen so much of her in recent years but she made a very important and rather wonderful part of my Baltimore past, and Dr. Marian Walker and I were talking of it all and of her in it when she was here just a couple of months ago, and so strangely enough Claribel had been very near me this last summer, and now Etta you know how I understand your loss and feel for it, do take my love and my fondest thought of Claribel

> Always,
> Gertrude

197

Tuesday November 5 1929—Hotel Lutetia
Dear Gertrude:

I do appreciate your understanding sympathy. Your realization of my sister is also a comfort to me. She always admired you profoundly.

I should like so much to hear you talk of my sister, some day when I am more calm within.

I thank you for your very kind letter. With my love for you and Alice I am

Your sincere friend
Etta Cone

While Etta waited to begin her sadly burdened journey back to Baltimore, the Baltimore newspapers were writing politely about Claribel's death. Her will had not yet been made public.

Appropriately, New York Harbor was deeply swathed in a thick, white, almost Wagnerian fog when they arrived. The *Statendam* was delayed for many hours. At last it was able to berth in Hoboken. Julius, his wife Laura, and Mrs. Ceasar Cone met the boat. After a brief reunion they boarded the train to Baltimore. Claribel's body had been placed aboard the train. After a subdued dinner they arrived in Baltimore around ten o'clock. Although the others were reluctant, Etta insisted that the burial service for Claribel be conducted that same night. The party went directly to the family mausoleum, where they were met by a rabbi. Except for a kerosene lantern there was no light in the mausoleum.

When Etta returned to the Marlborough her first task

was to assure herself that the museum was in good order. Then she spoke to her servants and decreed that Claribel's clothes were to be hung permanently in her cupboard. Etta also made clear that nothing was to be changed in the museum; the maid was to keep it immaculate and to display fresh flowers every day. There hung *The Blue Nude,* its violence accentuated by its presence among so many classical objects. There hung *Mont Ste. Victoire.* In those five rooms Claribel Cone's final statement, clear and measurable, stood for all the world to read.

On November 22, 1929, the *Sun* carried a story headed "Cone Art Unit May Pass to City Museum":

. . . the possibility that the widely known art collection of the late Dr. Claribel Cone, Baltimore scientist and art connoisseur, eventually will pass as a unit into the keeping of the new Municipal Museum of Art, together with a fund of $100,000 for housing, preserving and maintaining the collection was learned yesterday.

Under the terms of Dr. Cone's will, filed late yesterday, the large accumulation of paintings, chiefly by famous leaders and representatives of modern schools, of textiles, objets d'art, furniture, etc., may be acquired by the museum after the death of Dr. Cone's sister, Miss Etta Cone, or in the latter's lifetime if this should be her wish. It is suggested, however, that this may be done if "the spirit of appreciation of modern art in Baltimore becomes improved."

Determination of this last, as in fact, of all other related matters, is in the hands of the sister in whose keeping the collection is left.

An editorial also appeared in the *Sun* the same day:

Dr. Cone's doubts about the city's cultural zeal can be understood by anyone who realizes, for example, how few in the city even knew of the notable collections which she and her equally devoted sister had painstakingly assembled, or knowing, realized how enormous a part of Baltimore's total art resources they amount to. The ultimate bestowal of these works— in certain phases of truly national importance—upon the Museum depends definitely on Miss Etta Cone's conviction that the community deserves them and wishes them. How that can be evidenced is something about which the community in general and the Museum in particular should promptly bestir themselves. We are wisely required to prove our worth before we are given this spirited stimulus toward our artistic renaissance.

When a Baltimore *Sun* reporter finished an awed tour of Miss Etta's apartment and had seen Dr. Claribel's museum, Etta sat at her desk holding the letter Henri Matisse had written her in Paris. She translated the letter aloud. Then Etta spoke of a conversation she had overheard between Dr. Claribel and Matisse at a dinner party.

"Art and its appreciation are a God-given gift," Claribel had said to Matisse.

"Yes," he had answered, "but sometimes the artist has to descend to hell to get it."

Claribel Cone left for herself what might have been a suitable epitaph in one of her numerous notebooks. It is a fragment she had copied in 1927 from a book by Christian Brinton illustrated by Felix Vallotton.

Search where you may,
Choose what you will
There lurks at the bottom of
    all the world holds of beauty and sublimity
A touch of the sardonic.

It is the question mark
    which Satan places after
every deed however noble
At the end of each life
however divinely lived.

Five

Baltimore: "The Spirit of Appreciation"

NOW ETTA HAD TO FACE life alone. Her companion in collecting, her correspondent who wrote her daily letters, her tormentor, her partner in discussing everything from prices to personalities, was gone. She was forever alone. As she sat day after day in her apartment, unable to accept the friendship and interest brought by visitors, only one warmth reached her. Alone, she walked silently through the apartments and looked at one and then another of her paintings, each loved, each chosen through love, and they comforted her. She would unlock Claribel's museum and, walking swiftly past the closet holding Claribel's clothes, take comfort in looking at all that Claribel had loved. Gradually Etta warmed again to life and knew that she would have to go on doing alone what they had always done together. By the spring of 1930 she was making plans to go to Europe for the summer.

She knew she could not go back to Lausanne. Even the thought of it was painful. Paris was all right, but she was too weary and too full of memories to spend a summer there. Where to go after Paris? Where could she go and be able to talk with someone who also loved paintings and would talk about them with her?

The National Hotel in Lucerne faces the picture-postcard view of Lake Lucerne and Mount Pilatus which have made this city popular as a resort. The National Hotel is an imposing building, with the kind of furnishings one expects of a first-class hotel. Etta stayed there in the summer of 1930; not for the view, which did not particularly interest her, but because it was directly across the street from Galerie Rosengart. The proprietor, Siegfried Rosengart, was her second cousin. His grandmother, Caroline, a sister of Herman Cone, had married Joseph Rosengart.

Claribel Cone had known Siegfried during her World War I years in Munich—but she seemed then strictly interested in medical affairs, and he was too young to be interested in Claribel. In the early 1920s Rosengart had become a partner in the Gallery Tannhäuser in Berlin and had established a branch of that gallery in Lucerne. Later he opened his own gallery in the same city. During the 1920s he saw the Cone sisters in Paris, where he sometimes had dinner with them at the Brasserie. He had occasionally seen them in Lausanne, and one day ran into them unexpectedly at a Gauguin show at the great art museum in Basel. "Come to dinner tonight," they said. "Where?" said Rosengart. "Why at our hotel in Lausanne, of course," was the reply. These two heavy, not young women had taken a four-hour train ride to see paintings in Basel and would reverse the procedure to return to Lausanne that same day. It would never occur to them that someone considerably younger was not up to such a strenuous day.

The warm feeling between Siegfried Rosengart and Etta Cone came only in part from their blood relationship—it was based more on their shared love of paintings. Rosengart, a tall, quick, enthusiastic man, thought of paintings much as others think of children. "You are connected to them," he would say. Etta felt the same way. After she settled down in the National Hotel, every morning at eleven o'clock she would arrive at Galerie Rosengart to talk to Siegfried. These visits of hers were heaven-sent for Etta's traveling companions, since it gave them the only free time they had away from her. They were a great pleasure to Rosengart. Etta Cone was the kind of collector he enjoyed. He had known collectors of all types—those who like to have very important collections, and the other kind, a smaller group, people who were fond of art and who never bought a painting just because it was important. Rosegart knew from many years' experience that one type of collector puts his pictures in front and himself stands in the background; the other type of collector poses in front of his collection and places the pictures in the background. Rosengart felt that the Cone collection was never subordinated to its owners. He knew the Cones bought only pictures that gave them excitement; if something interested either sister she had to get it. It was the same with their laces and jewelry. "Etta bought because she couldn't resist," he would say. To Rosengart, Etta was special. Many people look at pictures in galleries and go into museums, but it is a small part of their activities. For Etta Cone, life was art and her collection. Of his cousin he said, "Etta Cone had an enormous feeling for the quality of pictures. She was not like a connoisseur—not like an art historian. You can see it also in her feeling for laces—not only in pictures. There are hundreds interested in art who don't even look at laces. She and her sister—they had a *feeling* for it. I don't think in the beginning they had the idea of making a collection—it became one. Etta admired a great cathedral as much as a modern painting. She was not like a tourist. She had a special gift for feeling and seeing."

Siegfried Rosengart felt that Etta Cone's Matisse collection was a unique collaboration with the artist. He knew that Matisse saved two or three paintings each year especially to show Etta Cone. "Matisse liked her very, very much—he was glad to help her make a collection of his works. Matisse knew Etta Cone was coming each year in June—he would keep three paintings aside.

Perhaps she didn't like one. Out of the two remaining, she would ask Matisse to choose one. 'What would you like us to have in our collection?' she would ask Matisse. Of course, if she didn't like one, she wouldn't have bought it. She was too close to her collection to buy what she didn't like.

"You liked Etta Cone," Rosengart remembers. "She was a wonderful person. It was a kind of love—to speak about art—to be together—to have the same interests. If she was interested in somebody she was very nice. If not, not impolite but standoffish. With companions— it was difficult. If things were not arranged to her liking she was disagreeable."

So each summer from 1930 to 1935 Etta spent at least a month in Lucerne. The visitors were further enlivened by visiting with other collectors. The wife of Dr. Arthur Hahnloser, an oculist living in Winterthur, also collected paintings. She and Etta took to each other with great warmth. Every season Siegfried Rosengart would drive Etta to see Madame Hahnloser and her collection. The two had a spirit of collecting that was very much the same. Not only had they collected many of the same artists—Van Gogh, Cézanne, Matisse, Bonnard, Vuillard—but Madame Hahnloser had a Matisse oil of a pewter jug almost like the one Etta Cone owned. The visits were, of course, returned and Madame Hahnloser would come to see Etta at the Hotel National.

Another art collector Etta used to visit when she was staying in Lucerne was Mrs. Sidney Brown, of Baden. When a collector comes to visit another collector and says, "Oh, the Renoir is beautiful—the Cézanne superb!" a lovely friendship is usually born.

Whether Rosengart and his wife Sybil visited Etta of an evening, or Etta went to talk to Siegfried at his gallery, "she was always speaking about pictures. Pictures she saw here, elsewhere. She would come with a catalogue to discuss an exhibition she had seen—and would speak about each painting in the catalogue."

Rosengart observed that scenery did not interest Etta; she spoke to him only of music and art. Her musical tastes were confined to composers of her own generation, such as Brahms and Rachmaninoff.

Etta never asked Rosengart to show her anything particularly. Rather, he would hunt out art he thought she would enjoy. She bought her Gauguin oil, *Woman with Mango,* which had once belonged to Edward Degas, through Rosengart. The painting arrived at the gallery the day before Etta was scheduled to leave Lucerne for an auto tour of the Dolomites. She saw the sumptuous oil of a Tahitian woman dressed in a blue robe, holding a pink fruit, surrounded by a deep yellow background, and knew she must have it. She went away finally, to spend a sleepless night considering the purchase. The price was $15,000, more than she had ever paid for a painting before. Early the next morning she went to the gallery and bought the picture.

Her party left Lucerne. Etta had been worried about subjecting her heart to the strain of driving over a high mountain pass on their route. In her excitement over

her new Gauguin she sat quietly in the car, not noticing
the spectacular scenery. Finally she turned to her sister-
in-law Laura and said, "When are we going over that
high pass?" "We went over it an hour ago," Laura answered. When the party stopped for the night Etta
phoned Lucerne to tell Rosengart how happy she still
was that she had bought the painting.

After the Gauguin oil, Rosengart found Etta a Renoir
bronze (it was the third she bought); Picasso's *Study
for Family of Saltimbanques*; a charming *Mother and
Child,* an oil Picasso had painted in the 1920s. Etta had
avoided buying Picasso for over twenty years; she truly
did not believe he was earnest about his cubist painting.
The classic, light charm of *Mother and Child* appealed
to Etta as much as her early Picasso drawings. She also
bought a Manet pastel, *Lady with a Bonnet,* a Degas
pastel, *Dancer,* and an early Van Gogh oil, *Landscape
with Figures,* from her cousin. Rosengart found on each
occasion that Etta was very quick about making up her
mind—once she saw a painting she liked, she knew that
was what she wanted.

Although Rosengart had never been to America, he
knew which paintings Etta owned because she had
brought him photos of her apartment which showed
the various paintings clearly. So he knew what was in
the collection, and also that it was an important one.
He said to Etta one day, "Why don't you make a catalogue of your collection?" "Oh no," fussed Etta, "I
could never do that—it is too much for me."

This was Etta's invariable reaction to work involving minute detail—it was one of the reasons why she always preferred to travel with a companion. It was a necessity for her to have someone to arrange the small details of life, such as pinning each pleat in her dresses when it was time to pack and folding great quantities of tissue paper around them.

"I will do the catalogue with great pleasure," Rosengart volunteered. "Send me the photographs of the drawings and I will have it made for you."

Slowly, after Etta returned to Baltimore in 1932, photos of the paintings arrived in Lucerne. She forgot to send the measurements, and Rosengart had to write for them. Etta made no pretense of being an art historian—she had few scholarly notes on the paintings she owned. Rosengart had to read catalogues and art books to get the necessary information for the catalogue. Everything went along fairly smoothly until Etta sent him a photo of the flower painting by Van Gogh that she had bought in New York at the Reinhardt Gallery. After some deliberation Rosengart wrote back that he could not reproduce the Van Gogh in the catalogue because he doubted its authenticity. Etta was shocked by her cousin's doubts, although she had had some intimation from various articles she had read. The following summer she spent weeks traveling to Holland to see Vincent Van Gogh, Theo's son, who would say only that he had never seen the painting before. Next she took it to a Van Gogh expert to whom the painter's nephew sent her—a Dr. De Wild, who told her emphatically that it was a fake; he even knew the man who had forged it. Etta asked him what she should do with the painting, since the gallery had closed. Dr. De Wild asked, "Do you like the picture?" Etta said yes. "Then hang it and enjoy it," Dr. De Wild said.

Etta wrote later of this to Rosengart: "Did I write you that Dr. De Wild's decision was against the Van Gogh flower picure? I cannot be too sad, for I have the lovely one from you and the *Shoes*."

Another difficulty in producing the catalogue arose when, after Rosengart had engaged what he considered the best printer in Europe—Ganymed in Berlin—Hitler took over the German government. Etta was very upset that her catalogue would have any connection with Hitlerite Germany, but it was too late to stop production. Rosengart prevailed on the printer to leave out his imprint. (It was a painful experience for Rosengart too. His sister and nephews were forced to flee Germany because of Hitler's persecution of the Jews. Etta's brother Julius and his wife Laura signed affidavits guaranteeing the welfare in America of Rosengart's family.) When the catalogue, a large, handsomely designed, heavy book in tan linen, was almost finished, Rosengart suggested to Etta that they print an additional five hundred copies to sell. She would not even consider the idea. She wanted only enough to send to museums, universities, libraries, and other collectors. Her wishes were respected. Since the catalogue was printed on circular rotogravure plates which were then destroyed, the thousand-odd copies of this book are all that will ever be printed. The first page reads:

THIS CATALOGUE
is dedicated to the memory of
DR. CLARIBEL CONE
by her sister Etta Cone

The title page reads:

THE CONE COLLECTION
OF BALTIMORE MARYLAND
CATALOGUE
OF PAINTINGS—DRAWINGS—SCULPTURE
OF THE NINETEENTH AND TWENTIETH
CENTURIES
WITH A FOREWORD BY GEORGE BOAS

The back of the title page says:

PUBLISHED AND COPYRIGHTED 1934 BY
ETTA CONE—BALTIMORE—MARYLAND
—U.S.A.

One hundred and twenty-five plates follow. Matisse and Picasso of course dominate the catalogue, but the long alphabetical list of artists includes: Boas (Dr. Boas' sculptor wife, Simone Brangier Boas), Boudin, Brenner, Cézanne (Etta now owned a Cézanne oil of *Bathers* as well as Claribel's *Mt. St. Victoire*), Chirico, Clark, Coubine, Courbet, Cross, Dalou, Degas, Derain, Despiau,

Friesz, Van Gogh, Guggenheimer (her cousin Richard, who studied with Coubine), Hyatt, Kisling, Kroll (Leon Kroll, the American artist), Laurencin, Maillol, Manet, Marquet, Matisse (thirty-one oils, one water color, ten pages of Matisse drawings and eighteen of Matisse's bronzes are listed). Next, Jean Matisse, the sculptor's son. Etta had bought two of his bronzes. The list included Monet, Morisot, and then Picasso. He is represented by one painting, six gouaches, four water colors, one sepia, twenty-four drawings, and one bronze. (Many of the drawings were those Etta or Claribel had bought off his studio floor that winter of 1905–6.) Also Pissarro, Redon, Renoir (Etta owned seven Renoir oils and one bronze). Next is Theodore Robinson. (He is represented in the catalogue by *Girl in Woods, Mother and Child, Horse Drinking, Girl with Violin*—the first paintings Etta owned; she had bought them in 1896.) The list continues with Rodin, Sheldon, Signac, Silbert (Ben Silbert was a painter Etta liked personally; she bought many of his paintings, trying to help him). Sisley, Stevens, Vallotton, Vlaminck, Zak, and Zorach complete the list.

In listing some of the titles and attributions of the paintings to previous owners Etta had her silent revenge for the condescension she had long suffered from Gertrude Stein. Vallotton's *Portrait of Gertrude Stein* is listed merely as *Portrait de G. S.* The famous 1906 Picasso portrait of Leo Stein is *Portrait de L. S.* Etta had bought Leo's portrait from Gertrude in 1932. Of

215

all the various paintings that Claribel and Etta bought from Gertrude Stein—the Picasso *Woman with Bangs,* the Cézanne *Bathers,* the Marie Laurencin *Group of Artists,* the Picasso mask *Head of Man,* even the notoriously famous *Blue Nude*—no mention is made that they once hung at 27 Rue de Fleurus, although Etta acknowledged in print that John Quinn had owned *The Blue Nude.* The essential characteristic of a "lion" is to deny the existence of any others, and after thirty years of learning by example from Claribel and Gertrude, Etta, with the publishing of her catalogue, became a "lion" too.

When Etta inscribed a copy to Siegfried Rosengart, she wrote: "To my dear cousins Sybil & Siegfried Rosengart with gratitude and recognition of my Cousin Siegfried's work as compiler of this catalogue. Etta Cone."

In 1932 Rosengart and his wife celebrated the birth of their only child, a daughter they named Angela. Etta Cone fell in love with the little girl. Each year she arrived from Paris with elaborate gifts for Angela. One year Etta brought her a handsome blue coat with gold buttons. Angela liked it so much she felt she ought to give Etta a gift in return. She bestowed a slightly used doll on her cousin Etta, which Etta took back to Baltimore.

When Etta was sailing home the following year, Angela gave her a batch of her child's drawings. Etta wrote to Siegfried from aboard the Holland-America ship: "Tell Angela I love her drawings and she must not forget me. I will soon see my little doll that Angela gave me last year."

Life had by no means proved to be as empty as Etta thought it would be. The winter of 1930 in Baltimore turned out to be one of the most exciting of Etta's life. The story was told simply on two pages of her desk calendar:

> December 17 1930—Morning 11:45 Mons. Henri Matisse arrives
> Afternoon: Lunch with Mons. Matisse
> Evening: Philharmonic—Mons. Matisse as guest
> December 18, 1930
> Morning: 10:42—Mons. Matisse left for New York

Mons. Matisse—her artist, her great one—had come to visit Etta Cone and stay a night in the apartments where his paintings had been hanging for over twenty years. Fred graciously gave up his apartment for the distinguished guest.

Henri Matisse had come to America to be a juror at the Carnegie International in Pittsburgh where he helped award the first prize to Picasso. Matisse also wished to see his paintings which Dr. Barnes had hidden in his Merion, Pennsylvania, retreat. They were hidden from the public, that is. Only those whom Dr. Barnes found worthy were allowed to see his tremendous collection of Matisses, Cézannes, and Renoirs. Dr. Barnes had asked Matisse to undertake the creation of lunettes to decorate his exhibition hall and Matisse was intrigued with the challenge. Nonetheless, Matisse found it relaxing to leave Merion for Baltimore and visit with Etta Cone.

It is not hard to imagine Etta's preparation for the master's visit—planning menus, overseeing the dusting and polishing, then her final walk through the three apartments, checking that all was in readiness. Nor is it hard to guess at Matisse's pleasure in viewing his paintings in such a warmly homogeneous setting. When he entered her apartment and saw the paintings, the big, brightly polished French brass milk urns filled with fresh flowers, with the best altar cloth on the dining table, Etta resplendent with a magnificent lace collar over her usual dark dress, a string of coral beads added for color, Matisse stepped once more into the world of Paris. It reminded him of Sally's and Michael's home— and yet it was a distinctive setting. It was Etta Cone's apartment. Next door there were those powerful paintings of Matisse's earlier years—*The Blue Nude* and *The White Turban* reminded him of the good Dr. Claribel. Etta and Matisse walked quietly and reflectively through Claribel's apartment. When the two reached the door and stood there a minute as Etta locked it, she could not help saying how much it would have meant to Claribel to see Matisse here, among the paintings, his and hers.

The artist and his admiring patron talked about a project that had been discussed by mail. Etta deeply regretted that Matisse had not made a drawing of her sister during her lifetime. It would have meant so much to Etta. Matisse had sent an alternate suggestion through his daughter Margot, who handled a great deal of his correspondence. She had written Etta in November 1930, "My father has asked me to say how sorry he is that circumstances prevented him from doing a portrait of Dr. Claribel Cone. He thinks it would be possible, thanks to his very lively memory of her, to do a drawing which, while not a portrait, would be the expression of his memory of her personality. He asks that you Miss Cone, collect all possible photos of Claribel Cone so that he can choose from among them when he comes to you in Baltimore in December."

So the photographs of the dead sister were given to the artist, who said he would like to do a drawing of Mademoiselle Cone too, if that would please her. It would please her very much, and she would look forward with the keenest anticipation to seeing the finished drawings.

Matisse's visit did not go unnoticed by the Baltimore press. The *Sun* ran an editorial, implying that if Matisse wanted to do some paintings of Baltimore it was all right. Edmund Duffy, the newspaper's cartoonist, did his impression of a typical Matisse window composition. Through the window could be seen, slightly atilt, supposedly in the modern manner, Baltimore's houses with their white steps. The cartoon was captioned, "Charles Street Evening—or Matisse Comes to Baltimore (With Respectful Apologies)."

A. D. Emmart of the Baltimore *Sun* was given the

privilege of interviewing the now acknowledged "old master" at Etta's apartment. Matisse would not discuss his contemporaries. He preferred to talk of his liking for America. Emmart wrote:

America impressed M. Matisse. Its extensiveness, its variety and the quality of its light. He thinks, moreover, that it promises to develop a school of painting of its own, but he believes that now this is still in process of development and little therefore can be said of it. But he feels American painters should deal with America. They may study abroad and take what they can from Europe. It is in America, finally, and out of America that they must take their pictures.

Emmart described Matisse's appearance at that time:

He is 61 years old now, but he moves and speaks with a restraint of energy and economy of gesture which speak of great vital resources. He is a short and compact figure, very straight-shouldered, and almost —in quite the best sense—military in bearing. His hands are like hands of a sculptor; his eyes as steady as those of a marksman.

Taking his leave of Etta, Matisse spoke of hoping to see her in Paris or Nice before long. He also promised to undertake the portraits of the Cone sisters at the earliest opportunity.

After Etta's beautiful catalogue had been studied by the art experts, the number of pilgrims traveling to see the Cone collection increased. Now well-known museum directors, curators, critics, and painters on both sides of the Atlantic wrote Etta months in advance to request an audience and the privilege of seeing her collection. She was gracious always, opening her door to anyone who had asked for admittance in an appropriate fashion. She frequently invited one of the important visitors to join her and her brother Fred for a delicious lunch. Her mailbox now was crowded with effusive notes expressing the gratitude of well-known art figures. If Etta liked a visitor particularly and knew he had not yet received her catalogue, she would later send a copy as a sign that the visitor had found favor with her.

Since there was still a reasonable doubt about where the collection would ultimately go, a number of interested museum directors managed to keep in touch with Etta in a discreet fashion. One of these, who had good reason to consider modern art his special province, sent Etta friendly postcards from scenic spots in Europe when he was vacationing, assuring Miss Cone that he and his wife were thinking of her often. The director had once been heard to say he thought the Cone collection was too good for Baltimore. Fortunately for her fellow citizens, Etta's devotion to her home city was unshakable and she felt a deep interest in the growing Baltimore Museum. She was aware that the museum staff had an excellent appreciation of her paintings. She also knew that they never ceased their efforts to educate the people of Baltimore to twentieth-century art, American as well as European. The museum had its share of critics who, like the earlier delegations to the Baltimore *Sun,* would demand the scalps of those at the museum responsible for showings of modern paintings. The demands were set forth clearly in vituperative letters addressed to the museum's director after each show the public considered outrageous. Fortunately the abuse did not alter the museum in its course. Rather, it spurred those concerned to further educational efforts: the need for them was so clear.

As late as 1929 there had been reverberations similar to the Shelby Shackleford affair of 1925, when an Institute student was denied a showing of her work because it was too modern. The director of the Maryland Institute, Hans Shuler, then saw fit to fire a popular painting instructor, Charles Walther. Again it was for "modernist tendencies." Henry Adams, president of the board of directors of the Maryland Institute, was interviewed by a *Sun* reporter on the matter. The reporter wrote:

> Mr. Adams specifically refused to say that Mr. Walther was dismissed because he didn't draw trees as they actually were in Nature. He limited himself to saying that some modernists did that. So far as his personal preferences were concerned, Mr. Adams said he preferred human bodies which looked like human bodies and trees which looked like trees. . . . "Some of the modernistic painters of Germany" said Mr. Adams, making it clear that in all this he was expressing his own point of view and not that of the board "paint figures that are outrageous."

"Was Mr. Walther dismissed because he drew such figures?" Mr. Adams was asked.

"I don't think that was his department," he answered. "He painted landscapes."

The *Sun* came out editorially regretting the dismissal of Charles Walther. Dr. George Boas gathered the facts of the case and wrote a pamphlet on the incident. These gestures notwithstanding, Walther was never reinstated. He was a man of considerable patience and through the mid-1930s he continued to prod the museum or the Maryland Institute through lengthy and detailed letters to the newspaper whenever he felt the horizon for artists was closing in again in Baltimore.

The foregoing does not mean that twentieth-century art won quicker acceptance elsewhere in the United States. Since the now powerful Museum of Modern Art did not open its doors until the autumn of 1929, Baltimore seems to check out as being even slightly in the vanguard of acceptance. The presence of the Cone collection in Baltimore no doubt helped to hasten the day of recognition.

The summer of 1932 saw Etta initiating one of her nephews into the pleasures of European travel. Harold Cone, a talented young music student, was the son of Etta's younger brother Bernard, who took care of Etta's finances for her. She always agonized over what Bernard would say when she purchased another expensive painting, although it was her own money she was spending.

She had often told her brothers, a little defensively, "I bet my paintings will turn out to be better investments than *your* investments."

The summer with her nephew Harold might have gone off smoothly, but Miss Kaufman was not available to travel with Etta and had recommended a nurse friend as substitute. Miss Bowman was well-intentioned and efficient, but Etta's requirements for a companion were beyond her abilities. Etta could not forgive the nurse her inability to distinguish between Notre Dame and Sacré Coeur, even after a month in Paris. Young Harold was excited by all Etta showed him on their travels but felt somewhat embarrassed to witness scenes when Etta vented her displeasure on the hapless Miss Bowman.

In the autumn of 1932 Etta wrote to acknowledge a copy of Gertrude's manuscript, *Two Women,* which Gertrude had signed and forwarded to Baltimore:

"My dear Gertrude: I was much moved at your remembering my sister as you did, and I shall catalogue your manuscript among her other art books which eventually will go to a museum—no doubt the Museum of Baltimore.

"I thank you profoundly for this generous tribute to my sister's memory. Life continues very empty without her but I am trying to carry on as she would have wished done. The Picasso picture of Leo will be an important addition to those we had and I am very glad to have it.

"I am also happy to add your new books to those who collect them in Baltimore—among whom, as you no doubt know, is George Boas of Johns Hopkins University. Yours, Etta Cone."

Gertrude replied to Etta promptly. "My dear Etta: I liked very much what you told me of Dr. Boas, it means a lot to me, we are getting ready a volume of operas and plays, I often think of Claribel in connection with all this; I know how much she would have delighted in the books and in the proofs—my poor Etta I do realize how lonely you are without her, she was so tremendously real direct and alive, I was very fond of her, my dear. A great deal of affection for you. Always, Gertrude."

When Etta was ready to go abroad for the summer of 1933 her party included her brother Julius' wife, Laura, and her two children, Edward and Frances. Edward was a gifted young pianist. Laura had been a family favorite of Etta's for some time, and she had grown even closer after Claribel's death. Laura could speak directly to Etta, without any reticence or subterfuge, and although Etta would not accept such frankness from just anyone, she enjoyed it in Laura.

Etta's French was the occasion for a pleasant little family conspiracy. While they were crossing on the *Statendam*, Etta said to young Edward, "Now let's correct each other every time we make a mistake in French." Edward, an excellent language student, found many occasions to correct Etta's pronunciation and vocabulary. Etta found no opportunities to correct Edward. After a few days Laura drew her son aside and advised him just to forget about the arrangement; it was bound to prove upsetting to Etta. So Edward stopped correcting Etta, who finally commented, "You see, my French has improved so much you don't find anything left to correct. I told you all I needed was a little practice."

Etta wrote to Gertrude from aboard the *Statendam* in June 1933: "My dear Gertrude: I was very much flattered to see from your *Autobiography of Alice Toklas* that you remembered my one time remark as to my 'ability to forgive but not forget.' I haven't changed. Those were wonderful days. . . . I am traveling abroad with my sister-in-law Laura and her children this summer. . . . It is delightful to read your story in the *Atlantic Monthly*. With love for Alice and much for you I am, Your sincere friend, Etta Cone."

Encouraged by the seeming friendliness of Etta's tone, Gertrude wrote Etta from her summer home, in the department of Bilingnin in Ain, later in the summer:

"Dear Etta: If you should be coming back this way from Italy and it is a pleasant way to come we would be very pleased to see you. If you are near Geneva or Aix le Bains, it is all very near us, and we would be very glad to have you and your family lunch with us. It is lovely here. . . . I hope you are thoroughly enjoying yourselves, it is a very lovely summer, Always, Gertrude."

Two weeks later Etta replied en route in her travels to Gertrude's invitation:

"Dear Gertrude: Your very kind letter followed us. . . . I thank you for your kind invitation for my family and me, but as our route from here will be directly to

Paris, we shall not be able to accept, and I am sorry. . . .
Your autobiography of Alice Toklas is one of the most
interesting and the best of the literature of today. With
all good wishes for your continued success I am as always, Your sincere friend, Etta Cone."

Although Etta would not move ten steps out of her
way for Gertrude any longer in spite of her always gra-
cious-seeming letters, she had made a long, wearying
trip to Nice, hoping to see Matisse. Her patience was
richly rewarded. She described the visit in a letter to her
brother Fred:

> Hotel Negresco
> 37 Promenade des Anglais
> Nice
> July 22, 1933

Dearest Fritz:

. . . Our three days here have been perfect. We
found, after going out to Cap Ferrat, where Matisse
was summering, that an illness made him return to
Nice ten days ago. His wife was expecting to hear
from me and insisted (over the phone) that I come to
see her husband who was in bed but convalescing.

My visit was a joy. One of the first things he said
was: "When I am able to work the first thing I shall
do is to make the drawing of Dr. Cone," then he said,
"I have a surprise for you," and presently I turned
and there sat the model in the yellow taffeta dress
with the large yellow hat on, just in front of the window—the exact reproducion of my latest painting.
His bedroom (which is his atelier when he is well)

was the scene of this picture. Needless to say, I was thrilled.

Well, Mons. Matisse would not listen to my plan to leave Nice the next morning (today) for as he explained Marguerite would arrive demain and she would show me the original decoration for the Barnes Foundation. Also he insisted that Laura and the children come to see him this afternoon, so according to the master's voice, here we are. Poor fellow, he has had several stones in the kidney and says he has been over-fatigued. I know it was the result of his hard work. He again said how sorry he was not to have been able to visit you and me.

. . . Since writing the first page Madame Duthuit appeared on the scene and we . . . had a very good lunch at the hotel. Then Raymond took us to the studio where we saw the original design for Barnes' salon. It is a wonderful production and Laura and the children got great pleasure from seeing it. Next we went home with Madame Duthuit and my little family party was presented to Matisse, who was still in bed. We were having a very happy visit when the doctor came in. He begged us to await the doctor's departure, but he stayed too long, so we left. Marguerite is to come here for dinner. She is really being lovely to me. . . . Laura said . . . that she never saw me so excited as after my visits to Matisse. . . .

With heaps of love,

Etta

Matisse had to do the Barnes decorations twice because of miscalculations in size. He had traveled to

Merion to install them himself. Etta finally decided against buying the originals because of her tiny, cramped apartments.

Raymond, mentioned in Etta's letter to Fred, was Etta's regular chauffeur whenever she was in Europe. He drove an impressively large black Minerva and would meet Etta whenever she disembarked at Cherbourg or Le Havre. On one occasion, when the *Statendam* docked late because of fog, Etta fussed all during the drive to Paris because she was afraid the night clerk at the Lutetia would not know her.

Although Etta would not visit Gertrude Stein, she did make a point of visiting Leo and Nina Stein in Settignano on a number of her Italian tours. Leo and Etta had remained friends through all the years. Life had altered their original roles, when Leo was the teacher and Etta the eager student. Leo had been trying to paint for years but felt he had to cure himself of what he described as "crippling neuroses" before his work could fully develop. He had little success, financial or artistic, with his painting. Etta, now a well-known and well-to-do collector, always bought a number of Leo's paintings when she stopped to see him. Etta also enjoyed seeing Leo's wife Nina. She realized that Nina had given Leo what little happiness he had known.

During the early 1930s Etta bought a number of the most important paintings Matisse produced. One was the aforementioned *Girl in a Yellow Dress*. Later she bought the large and boldly designed *The Magnolia Branch,* which was a major effort. She also bought *The Pink Nude.* Matisse furnished her with a set of photos he had taken to show twenty-one different stages *The Pink Nude* had gone through. In 1932 Etta also purchased the maquette for Matisse's thirty etchings created to illustrate the *Poésies* of Mallarmé. Skira published the volume handsomely. The maquette included all the original drawings, as well as trial plates and proofs. Matisse had written to Etta, thanking her for her compliments on that work: "I was very pleased with your reaction to the volume and the rest of the set. I considered this work very complete and any real sympathy that it encounters means a lot to me. It means all the more when it comes from you who will remain close to the whole thing and have the possibility of seeing it again. . . . I hope that it is a new pleasure for you every time."

In the spring of 1934 Etta had written to Gertrude from Baltimore:

"Dear Gertrude: Last fall I wrote you a letter and then you became ill. In that letter I expressed admiration for your book, which as you know has become the most popular of the recent publications. I was deeply touched to find myself one of the characters, and what you said of my sister was beautiful and it grieves me that she cannot know what you thought of her.

"To my keen regret, my health prevented me from going to New York to hear your opera, but there is still hope that it may come here. Many museum directors have been here this winter and many of them were thrilled to find the bronze and portrait of you in this collection. I always apologize for the Vallotton portrait for it is not you. Valuable as is the *Autobiography of*

Alice Toklas now, I think there is nothing of today that can take its place in the future as a chronicle of the art of the first years of this century. . . ."

That autumn Etta learned that Gertrude and Alice, now very much in the literary limelight, were coming to America for a lecture series. Baltimore was on the itinerary. Etta, in spite of her refusal of Gertrude's invitation to visit at Aix, couldn't resist writing Gertrude, when she had arrived in New York:

"Dear Gertrude: I just heard through Hetty that Mrs. Stein was not able to have a reception for you on account of her husband's illness. Should you care to meet any people at my place I will gladly arrange it for you. Perhaps you would like to meet George Boas and others here interested in your work.

"Any other use you care to make of my small place it will be a pleasure to have you do. As I expect to go South I will appreciate your answer before making my date of departure definite. . . .

"Hoping to have the pleasure of entertaining you & Alice I am with love for you both, Sincerely, Etta."

Gertrude replied the next day:

> Hotel Algonquin
> 59 West 44th Street
> New York New York
> October 30, 1934

My dear Etta

Thanks so much for your invitation, but I am not accepting any invitations. There is so much more happening than in our wildest dreams, —I am simply seeing no one except a few very dear friends. As I am lecturing in Baltimore I will undoubtedly meet Dr. Boas and that will give me a great deal of pleasure, but you can understand that with lecturing, broadcasting, cinema newsreels and newspaper people and my editors, I must in between go very easy. But I do want to meet Dr. Boas and the others and that will come about naturally. . . . I am awfully sorry if you will not be in Baltimore when we get there, but some time we will meet. Always lots of love

Gertrude

Etta was not in Baltimore when Gertrude lectured. She had made an unexpected trip to Greensboro, which surprised her family there, since she had always before come only in the summertime. Gertrude and Etta never saw each other again, and Gertrude never saw the Cone collection at the Marlborough Apartments. Gertrude and Alice spent Christmas Eve in Baltimore with Zelda and Scott Fitzgerald and visited Gertrude's cousins living at nearby Pikesville.

Although Gertrude Stein's tour of America was a huge success, there were sounds of discontent from a number of the artists and writers Gertrude had written about in *The Autobiography of Alice B. Toklas.* The literary magazine owned by Eugene and Maria Jolas, *transition,* which published a number of pieces by Gertrude Stein, carried the comments of her critics in February 1935.

George Braque wrote of her: "Miss Stein understood nothing of what went on around her. I have no intention of entering into a discussion with her, since it is obvious that she never knew French really well and that was always a barrier. But she has entirely misunderstood Cubism, which she sees simply in terms of personalities. . . ."

Henri Matisse, who had broken with Gertrude Stein many years earlier, wrote an account in French which was translated: ". . . Miss Toklas, in other words, Miss Stein, has contacted indiscriminately things about which, it seems to me, she has understood nothing. . . . Her book is composed, like a picture puzzle, of different pieces of different pictures which at first, by their very chaos, give an illusion of the movement of life. But if we attempt to envisage the things she mentions the illusion does not last. In short, it is more like a harlequin's costume, the different pieces of which, having been more or less invented by herself, have been sewn together without taste and without relation to reality."

Leo Stein let it be known to interviewers that he considered the book a sort of romantic fiction.

It was a curious phenomenon that Etta, during the years after her sister's death, came to resemble Claribel. With Claribel gone, the attention accruing to the collection now was focused on Etta, and she loved it. She loved to tell her stories of the old days in Paris. It took her almost two hours to show the collection and tell her stories. Now it was Etta who sat spellbinding a roomful of attentive listeners. Too, her temper when she didn't get her own way reminded some of the family of the departed Claribel. It was noticed that, besides Claribel's gifts as a storyteller, Etta had taken on some of the characteristics of her sister which she had always deplored.

Etta was still shy about her physical appearance. She once remarked to Laura Cone, "Isn't it odd that someone who loves beauty as much as I do should look the way I look?"

Mrs. Adelyn Breeskin, who met Etta when she came to work in the Baltimore Museum in the early 1930s, and who remembered seeing Claribel at the Lyric concerts when she was a child, often came from the museum to visit. Mrs. Breeskin was now curator of prints and drawings at the museum. Etta invited her over for lunch every time she had a new painting. The two ladies would discuss the charms of the new work and where it should be hung in the tiny rooms. Although it made Mrs. Breeskin unhappy that the large Cézanne painting, *Mont Ste. Victoire,* was hung over a radiator in Claribel's museum, she could not say anything to its current owner, who had decreed that nothing was to be moved in Claribel's museum.

One afternoon Mrs. Breeskin, who often escorted guests of the museum to the Cone apartments, brought the painter Franklin Watkins to call. As Etta entered her living room to join the guests, she stood for a moment, majestically framed by the doorway. Watkins rose, exclaiming that he would like to paint her full length just as she stood there. He said she made a handsome, monumental figure. Although the meeting was a pleasant one, Mrs. Breeskin could never convince Etta that Watkins had sincerely admired her appearance, and the portrait was never painted.

Etta had a succession of young secretaries during those years, who were kept busy cataloguing laces and prints, sorting the triplicates of Claribel's art books or some similar task. They would lunch with her at the apartment every day. Lunch was a one-sided affair, since a twenty-year-old girl might find herself served a superbly prepared crab casserole, on the daintiest of china, while Etta ate a small portion of simple dairy food, necessary because of her chronic stomach difficulties. If the secretary was so ill-advised as to express an admiration for a particular dish, Etta might serve it for two weeks running. One young lady who was working for Etta, Gloria Lanier, told Etta she had never eaten Japanese persimmons before, and she found them delicious. Gloria ate them at Etta's for many days afterward. She was never able to bring herself to touch them again.

Leon Kroll, who lived in New York, came to Baltimore to teach at the Art Institute every other week. He was always a guest at Etta's table. He found the food excellent and the surroundings so charming that he was invariably late to class. Elinor Ulman, a second cousin of Etta's, was unofficial curator for Etta one season. When less "important" visitors were expected to see the collection, Etta would tell Elinor to show them around, but when the visitors actually arrived Etta could not bear to let another show the collection; she always did it herself. In February 1933 Etta wrote Mar-

235

got Matisse Duthuit that she was "always tired now from visits of artists and curators"—and although "contact with intellectuals gives me great pleasure, it prevents me from finishing my own work."

Etta finally had a clear mental picture of what her work was. She had set herself the goal, after she recovered somewhat from the loss of Claribel, of broadening the historical period her paintings covered. She wanted them to serve as a survey of nineteenth- and twentieth-century French painting. It was easier said than done. Even though she had plenty of money, it is not easy to find great paintings at any price. So she had friends in the art world on the lookout for her.

One was David Rosen, who "found" Etta her beautiful Corot *In the Studio*. Small-boned and German-born, Rosen had gone to Paris as a painting student in 1900. He had eaten ham and bread at the earliest Stein "open houses" at Rue de Fleurus. After he emigrated to America, Rosen began to work more as an art restorer than as a painter. He gradually achieved a reputation as one of the best in the country. He would come from his home in New York to Baltimore annually to do restoration work on the collections of the Walters Art Gallery. When he arrived Etta would telephone and say, "You're in Baltimore, for heaven sakes come to dinner." The dinner party would usually include Mrs. Adelyn Breeskin and Philip Perlman, a lawyer friend of Etta's who was Solicitor General of the United States. Etta invariably served the little group a chicken dinner.

Etta also took an interest in the Baltimore artists Aaron Sopher, Herman Maril, and Edward Rosenfield.

She bought 142 line and wash drawings from Sopher, who once asked permission to bring his two small daughters to see the collection. When the little girls came, Etta received them graciously and showed them around the apartments. The children were awed. One of the girls recovered her voice enough to say to Etta, "You've such beautiful things, what else could you want?" Etta answered, "One true friend."

Etta loaned her paintings and sculpture generously to the Baltimore Museum and made few demands on them. Considering that she was likely to be a future benefactor of theirs, she showed considerable breeding. The only time she ever threatened to take her treasures elsewhere was on the occasion of a loan show at the museum. She insisted that the employees of the local storage company who picked up the art objects from her apartment wear white gloves while moving the art. This made the museum people nervous, since they thought the white gloves slippery and ordinary hands much safer. There was no quarreling with Miss Etta's wishes, so white gloves were used by the burly moving man. After the show was over the art was returned. Etta, checking over each object minutely, found a few finger marks on the marble base of a head by Despiau. She called the museum in great anger, saying that greasy finger marks were all over her Despiau. She warned that she didn't have to leave her things to the museum if they couldn't take better care. Other than that one incident, she never used her collection to gain her own ends with the museum.

Two stories about Etta Cone and paintings—one

which she owned, the other one she could not bring herself to buy—indicate why the younger generation of her family and friends regarded her as prudish and Victorian.

Boy with Horse, one of Picasso's most fully realized paintings of the period when Etta first met him, came up for sale much later. Etta thought of buying the painting, but she didn't, though the price was reasonable. Years later she told her nephew Edward her reason for not buying it. The only place she could have hung it was in her dining room, and since the boy was nude, she was afraid it would disturb her dinner guests.

Knowing her attitude regarding the sanctity of her dining room, which she thought of as *the* Cone family dining room in Baltimore, Edward's father Julius once asked Etta about the Matisse she had hung behind her dinner table. It was one of the Matisse oils of the beach at Etretat, showing fish caught in a net, lying on the sand. Julius wanted to know if it didn't offend Etta to have dead fish in her dining room.

Etta is supposed to have answered, "I questioned Monsieur Matisse before I bought the painting, and he assured me he had a boy water the fish to keep them alive while he painted them."

It was such stories that made her nephews and nieces secretly decide that their aunt Etta was the most naïve lady alive.

Etta did nothing to clear up their confusion on how much she really "knew" about life. Just when they had finally decided she was hopelessly innocent, she would bring them up short once again with a story of some artist's mistress to whom she had taken a liking and whom she enjoyed as a dinner companion. It was a little hard for these young people who, along with many others of their generation, had embraced Matisse, Picasso, and Gertrude Stein as heroes, to accept the notion that their maiden aunt had been the friend of this trio of innovators for years and years. Certainly Etta contradicted, in her looks, in her speech, all that her juniors thought of as "modern." Yet there were those paintings on her walls—nobody could challenge *their* "modernity." It was all very perplexing. . . .

In 1936 Etta took Sister Carrie's granddaughter, Ellen Berney, to Europe with her. Ellen was just out of high school, quite interested in art, and extremely grateful to Etta for showing her around. The girl was thrilled to be taken to meet Matisse, who inscribed a drawing to her as a gift. Being a normally independent young lady of seventeen, Ellen did resent it somewhat when Etta would not let her niece use her own money even to buy postage stamps.

Henri Matisse had a studio in Paris that season. He invited Etta and her niece there for tea and also took tea with them at the Lutetia. His attentiveness extended to seeing that they were well entertained.

He wrote Etta a little note from his studio on Boulevard Montparnasse:

Dear Miss Cone,

Here are two tickets for a dance recital which will

certainly interest your niece and your protégé. I will take them if you would like me to.

Respectfully and devotedly,
Henri Matisse

132 Blvd. Montparnasse
Paris

I hope that Miss Ellen and your friend were able to see *Mutiny on the Bounty.*

Matisse and Etta had indulged in pleasant little social exchanges for many years, such as cabling each other birthday wishes. When Etta and Matisse parted after the summer of 1936 they exchanged hopes that the tragic drift of the world might improve. As it grew steadily worse, Etta no longer dared go abroad. She continued to collect paintings—buying her Matisses through his son Pierre or from Paul Rosenberg in New York—but she did not return to Paris.

In 1938 Michael Stein, who had resettled his family in California a few years earlier, died. Sarah and Etta exchanged mournful letters, each attempting to cheer the other, inevitably returning in the letters to remembrances of what had happened so long ago. Sarah's only remaining joy was in raising Daniel Stein, her grandson.

When World War II began, Gertrude Stein and Alice Toklas, who had finally left 27 Rue de Fleurus in 1935 for a larger apartment at 5 Rue Christine, stayed on at their country home, Bilignin. Later they moved to Culoz. Matisse disregarded the advice of his doctor and his children and insisted on staying in the South of France after

France fell. Leo and Nina Stein remained at their small villa at Settignano, above Florence. Leo, as he had grown older and very deaf, had miraculously become cheerful, vital, full of hope and plans. His ambitions now exceeded both his health and his life expectations. He was frantically busy painting and writing. He was on old man, a poor one too. He had finally published his first book in 1927—*The ABC of Aesthetics*. He was now working hard on his second book.

Matisse wrote intermittently to Etta during the war. In November 1939 he wrote, "One can never be entirely joyful, especially at the moment, when so many people are suffering. All one can do in the present emergency is try not to be utterly unhappy, simply not allowing oneself to be overcome by the terrible misfortunes of those whom we love, and be as active as possible to keep from thinking too much and losing courage. . . . Shall I tell you that I am always working—more than ever? What is better for making one forget about the present? We hope, dear Miss Cone, that all your family is well. Would you be so good as to give our regards to Fred—and as I don't know when you will get my letter I think I would do well to say now that we wish you a good Christmas and our very best for 1940, which, let us hope, will bring us Peace. As always, your devoted Henri Matisse."

Etta's pleasure had been further diminished by the death of her dear friend, Cecilia Gaul. Etta had quietly supported Miss Gaul during her last years. Now there was no one to play the piano with her. No trips to France. No visits with Monsieur Matisse. Her brother Fred died

in 1944, willing a few well-chosen paintings to the Balti-
more Museum. Fred had bought two Bonnard oils, a
Utrillo, a Rouault, and a Vuillard oil for his apartment.
He had also served on the board of the museum.

Out of touch as Etta was with the world at war, she had
her reasons to grieve too. Her loneliness was somewhat
lightened when a sympathetic friend in Baltimore introduced her to Lilly Schwarz, a German-born refugee piano
teacher. A widow in her forties, Lilly had no family, no
ties in America. She was able to give Etta the constant
attention Etta craved, and which Etta's large, busy family was unable to offer a woman in her seventies. So the
four-handed playing started for Etta again, and she attended concerts at the Lyric with her new friend. Etta
even had a trio of musicians come into her living room
and play, with Mrs. Schwarz at the piano; the slow movement of the *Archduke Trio* was Etta's favorite. She would
sit listening to the four musicians performing under the
paintings she loved, she would glance around her tiny
living room and know a few minutes of deep pleasure.

Another moment of real pleasure during the dreary
years came when Leo Stein sent Etta a copy of his second
book, published in 1947. It was titled *Appreciation:
Painting, Poetry and Prose.* Etta thought it excellent.
She had never ceased to credit Leo with stimulating her
interest in art. Just before his book was published she
had received a letter from Leo written in April 1947:

"Dear Etta: A letter from Fred Stein tells me that your
sympathy for our stummics has led you to make a contri-
bution for their amelioration. For this much thanks. We

have indeed been much dependent on supplies from America for during the last couple of years things have not been the least breezy over here. The only way to get decent milk is to make it oneself, that is, with powder, for the native product is a pale blue fluid with so very queer a taste that it spoils one's coffee. Nor can one buy good powdered milk here for all that is to be had is the half skimmed variety. . . . The only present return that I can make except this letter of thanks is to send you my book which is to appear very soon. All those who read the manuscript found it decidedly readable so I hope that you will too."

After discussing his wife's ill-health, Leo discussed his own: "Until lately I have been as usual or rather more so but then I developed some trouble in what you in certain unregenerate days under the influence of Gertrude's medical school terminology condescended to call a bum gut. Do you remember? . . ."

Leo closed his letter with ". . . My existence is so without incident that there is really nothing to write so I shall act as though that were really true and say no more. Cordially yours, Leo."

Three months later, in late July 1947, Leo Stein died in Florence. He outlived his sister—who had died in the American Hospital in Paris—by exactly one year and two days. They had never met again after their separation.

It was the summer of 1949. Etta had kept up her usual winter activities surprisingly—going to concerts and showing the still growing flood of visitors the art collection. Whenever Mrs. Breeskin, who had been director of the Baltimore Museum since the end of World War II, called to announce another visitor, Etta said, "Fine, but you know I can't talk to anyone. I'm not well enough— so you come and show them around." Invariably, when the guest arrived Etta would emerge and conduct the tour herself, telling the same loving stories of the paintings and painters again. With the coming of the summer months, Etta had to make plans for her summer, and they were difficult to make. She was seventy-nine years old.

She decided to go to Laura Cone at her summer home in Blowing Rock in the Blue Ridge Mountains—not far from where her brother Moses was buried on the grounds of his estate, Flat Top Manor. Laura, of all the family, had been a great comfort to Etta in recent years. She was deeply fond of her, and Etta responded with affection. At Blowing Rock that summer, Etta continued to do what she had always done. She made trips to the local linen shop, inspecting their wares with her magnifying glass as carefully as she had in Venice years ago. When her bill for linens that summer was tallied up, she had bought $1200 worth. One day Laura took her for a drive to see a young woman artist who had known the Cone family for many years. When Etta paid $1500 for a painting by the lady's husband, also an artist, Laura questioned her on her motives, since the painter was not particularly well known. Said Etta, "Brother Moses liked her when she was a little girl." Laura Cone's granddaughter, Little Laura, came to visit at the house with her parents. Every day Etta called the child to her side and let the three-year-old search through the contents of her pocketbook until she found the special gift Etta had tucked in for her.

One day late in August the little village telephone office of Blowing Rock was thrown into an uproar by its first telephone call from overseas. Somebody from Paris was calling the Cone household to speak to Miss Etta Cone. When the connection was made, Etta spoke to an ailing Allan Stein, son of Sarah and Michael, nephew of Leo and Gertrude. Allan Stein was sick in the American Hospital in Paris. And he was forced to sell paintings he had been given by his mother, who was still living in California, to meet the expenses of his illness. Did Miss Etta want to buy the gouache portrait that Picasso had done of him when he was a child? Miss Etta said she would have to think about it and call him back.

Paris . . . 1905 . . . the Luxembourg Gardens . . . Picasso's studio in Montmartre . . . the Rue Madame apartment . . . Madame Vernot . . . 27 Rue de Fleurus . . . Etta strolling with the boy Allan in the park, planning surprise treats for the long-ago Allan just as she now did for Laura's grandchild. Buying a new painting for the collection. But it wasn't new—she had seen it so long ago in Sarah's and Michael's apartment. . . . And now the boy was a sick man and wanted her to buy it—so that he could pay for sickness. . . . It was all so old and so new.

When Etta emerged from her room the following morning Laura noticed that she had brightened. There

245

was a gaiety in her voice. Laura asked her what she was going to do. A museum would offer him $20,000, Etta said, and a dealer would offer him $10,000—"I shall offer him $15,000 and he will take it." No wonder she looked brighter. Etta was off on the well-loved chase, on the scent of a new painting—yet not a new painting—a well-known painting that was somehow part of her life, part of the story. The telephone operators took it in their stride the second time around—they connected Miss Etta with the American Hospital in Paris in good order, and Miss Etta made her offer and Allan Stein accepted. He said he would also include as a gift three preliminary studies by Picasso. Miss Etta said good. Allan Stein said was there an American Express branch office in Baltimore that could forward the money to him, because he needed it as soon as possible. Miss Etta drew herself up and said sternly into the telephone that she did not deal with branch offices of American Express, she dealt only with the main one in New York, and they could be trusted to forward the money with dispatch. Allan Stein said that would be fine.

Etta then waited each day to see the picture. She had not seen it for many years, perhaps back in the late twenties or early thirties when the Steins were living at Garches. She remembered it well. Allan was in profile, about ten years old, his curly hair cut shorter than it had been when he wore his velvet suits walking with her in the parks of Paris. His lips were curled in that faintly knowing smile she had seen often on other Stein faces.

She made the time pass by visiting friends with Laura

and listening to her nephew Edward or Lily Schwarz play the piano.

At night, as she waited for sleep, she knew that she had been right—so long ago, when she bought her Robinson paintings and faced the ridicule of her family. She had said then what may have been her first independent thought—that the paintings would make their living room and perhaps their lives less drab. Now she was very old and alone. A tired sick man was sending her a painting of a young boy that would make life seem good and young and beautiful to her again. She would wait.

The painting took too long coming. When it arrived at the express office in Baltimore its new owner was dead of a heart attack which killed her on the last day of August 1949.

Epilogue

WHEN ETTA CONE'S DEATH was announced it was thought necessary to guard the apartments' collections, which the newspapers valued at $3,000,000. A Pinkerton guard was installed.

Then photographers came and took pictures of the rooms; an ironic finale for the apartments where the sisters had lived so quietly, Claribel for twenty years, Etta for forty. One photograph published in the *Sun* especially signaled the end of the sisters' privacy, for during their lifetime photographs of the apartments were not published. The newspaper photo showed Etta's bed and bedroom. It was subtle evidence that the Cone collections, created and cherished in privacy, were rapidly becoming public property.

The Pinkerton guard, who sat reading a detective magazine at a little table near the entrance of Etta's apartment, seized the chance to question Laura Cone about a Matisse painting one morning soon after Etta's funeral. He said he could not tell what the painting was about. After pointing out a bedridden figure in *The Invalid* to the bemused guard, Laura asked if he would like to see an even more puzzling picture. Laura and her son Edward, who had stayed in Etta's apartments while arrangements were being made for the funeral, led the guard to *The Blue Nude*. He stood dumb-struck before it, then finally muttered, "They don't need anybody to guard this place; nobody would steal that picture." That was the last time the famed blue lady sustained an insult as a private party—henceforth she belonged to the public. So did the rest of the Cone collection.

By the terms of Etta Cone's will, the entire collection was left to the Baltimore Museum and the City of Baltimore. The museum staff was free to take whatever paintings, sculptures, furniture, objets d'art, fabrics, and laces they considered of museum value and interest. The will named a committee to determine which items should be included in the bequest and which were to be excluded as duplicates or lacking in museum value. The committee consisted of the president of the Board of Trustees of the Baltimore Museum of Art; the director of the Museum, Mrs. Adelyn Breeskin; Laura Cone; David Rosen, the technical adviser of the Walters Art Gallery; and Philip B. Perlman, who was a member of the Board of Trustees of the museum. Perlman and the Safe Deposit and Trust Company of Baltimore were named as executors of the will. Etta also left $400,000 to build a wing to house the collection. That sum included $100,000 left by Claribel in her will for the same purpose.

Mrs. Breeskin and Dr. Gertrude Rosenthal, the senior curator of the museum, would supervise the transfer of the collections to the museum. It was not an enviable job. The apartments were jammed with the accumulation of two lifetimes devoted to collecting and shopping. End to end, the sisters had shopped for a total of eighty-five years, perhaps the longest and least-advertised shopping spree in the annals of American womanhood. Memories of lists in Claribel's little notebooks came alive through the apartments as the museum staff waded through cartons of Liberty scarves, ties, boxes of penwipers, pencil sharpeners, and note pads of all dimensions.

When they opened a cupboard in Claribel's apartment they were taken aback by the sight of her voluminous black dresses hanging fresh and neat. Etta had decreed they be preserved, and there they had hung for twenty years. Even after they had removed everything thought suitable for museum exhibition, the apartments seemed full. Next it was Laura Cone's job to give suitable remembrances of Etta to members of the family and friends. Etta's will had, of course, specified numerous money and stock bequests to her family, her charities, her traveling companions, and her servants. Her piano was given to her nephew Edward. Her music was to be shared by Mrs. Lilly Schwarz and her nephew Harold

Cone. Duplicates and triplicates of lithographs and etchings were given to the Women's College of the University of North Carolina.

Although Etta's table linens were distributed generously among numerous friends and relatives, enough still remained to supply the needs of Laura Cone's household indefinitely. Even after the museum had taken all the candlesticks of superior value, there were fifty-two pairs left. A Baltimore auction firm was finally called in to dispose of the formidable number of remaining objects. Only one restriction was put on the auction house; it was not permitted to mention the Cone family when it advertised the sale. Not until the auctioneers had removed all that was considered salable could the apartments finally be emptied.

Etta's death and gift to the museum put the story of the Cone sisters before the nation for the first time. Claribel's death and the terms of her will had been reported only in the Baltimore newspapers. It was a puzzling story. The sisters surely sounded quaint. Well-worn anecdotes were retold, including the story of Etta informing her brother that Matisse had hired a boy to water the fish so they would stay alive while he painted a beach scene. The sisters and their apartments were described as "Victorian." Yet the nation's magazines and newspapers were impressed with their modern art collection. It was acknowledged that the Cone sisters had turned out to be important art collectors, that their Matisse collection was one of international importance. The sisters were unlike the collectors the public knew about. Certainly they had very little in common with the great J. P. Morgan or Henry Clay Frick, or even with Mrs. Isabella Stewart Gardner of Boston, who had created a Venetian palace, Fenway Court, in Boston, to house her collections. The Cone sisters did not take on legendary stature; they seemed to be just what they had always been, two maiden ladies living in overcrowded small-roomed apartments in the Marlborough.

It was a classic case of the sum being greater than the parts. Until late in the 1920s the art world had not even thought of the Cones as serious art collectors. Their fellow Baltimoreans had considered the sisters to be eccentric, if not a little crazy. Now, in 1949, the newspapers were comparing their collection with the world's great Matisse collections: that of Dr. Albert Barnes at Merion, Pennsylvania; the collection in the Statens Museum in Copenhagen; and the Shchukin collection in Russia. The comparisons were certainly valid. The Cone collection contained forty-three Matisse oils, eighteen bronzes, and one hundred and thirteen drawings, as well as most of the master's graphic works. It provides a fifty-two-year chronology of Matisse's development, from 1895 to 1947.

When Henri Matisse came to the United States in 1930, he visited Dr. Barnes in Merion before going to Etta Cone in Baltimore. The order of the visits was logical. Dr. Barnes, buying rapidly in the 1920s from Michael Stein, from Tetzen Lund, the Danish collector, and from the Bernheim-Jeune gallery, had built the greatest Matisse collection in America. Alfred Barr, in his scholarly book on the artist, called Etta Cone's "the second most important Matisse collection in the country." Barr also wrote, "The Cone Collection includes forty-three Matisse paintings mostly of the Nice period but with several earlier works, among them 'The Blue Nude.' More remarkable still are the eighteen bronzes, one hundred thirteen drawings and hundreds of prints, groups, which, taken as a whole, far surpass those of any other museum." Their taste for Matisse was all the Cones and Dr. Barnes had in common.

Dr. Barnes, who made his fortune with the invention of a household medicine called Argyrol, was not a family friend of the Matisses. The paintings he bought were installed in the large two-story art gallery he had built adjoining his house on his Merion estate. There the paintings hung, viewed only by the doctor, his wife, and a chosen few. An ill-tempered man, Barnes was not interested in sharing his pleasures with strangers. The gates to the property were locked, and over the years only those who met Dr. Barnes's personal and arbitrary standards of appreciating art were allowed to see his huge collection of Renoirs, Matisses, and Cézannes. Such was the situation even after Dr. Barnes' death in 1951.

Not until March 1961 did the courts of Pennsylvania finally order the Barnes Foundation—which had been operating classes as a tax-exempt, non-profit institution —to open its doors to the public. At this writing, limited groups of two hundred a day are allowed in the art gallery, and thus far the courts have been promised only two viewing days a week by the reluctant trustees of the foundation.

The Barnes collection contains fifty-two Matisse oils, most of them large paintings created before 1925, including the famous *Joy of Life* of 1907. The Matisse decorations titled *Dance,* which the doctor commissioned from Matisse in 1930, are installed in the lunettes above the windows of the Barnes art gallery; the paintings, at their maximum dimensions, run some forty-five feet long and almost twelve feet high. The Barnes collection excites the connoisseur because of its heavy concentration on those periods considered to be the peaks of Matisse's originality—the Fauve paintings, others created between 1905 and 1910, and the austere, boldly designed paintings of 1916 and 1917.

Another great Matisse collection was the early one established by the Russian merchant, Sergei Shchukin, who bought heavily until around 1912. He had purchased such important paintings as *The Dinner Table* of 1908; *Portrait of Madame Matisse* of 1913; *Zorah on the Terrace* of 1912. He had commissioned Matisse to do decorations for his ornate Moscow mansion, and Matisse had created for him the *Dance* of 1909 and *Music* of 1910.

After the Communist revolution the collections of Shchukin and Morosov, another Moscow collector, were confiscated and their homes turned into museums by the Soviet government. In 1923 the two collections were merged into one magnificent collection known as the

257

Museum of Modern Western Art in Moscow. It contained forty-eight paintings and a few drawings. The paintings have since alternated between being stored in the museum basement and being hung with honor, depending on the politics of the hour. More recently, the collection has been divided again between two museums: the great Hermitage in Leningrad and the newly designated Pushkin Museum of Fine Art in Moscow. Since the end of the Stalin era, the Western visitor has had a better chance of seeing with his own eyes paintings he may have known only by reputation.

A third Matisse collection—sixteen paintings and a number of sculptures—is at the Statens Museum in Copenhagen. Its history is almost as ambiguous as that of the Russian collection. Before World War I, Michael and Sarah Stein were persuaded by Matisse to send important paintings from their collection to Germany for a big Matisse exhibition at the Gurlitt Gallery in Berlin. When the war began the paintings were confiscated by the Germans as enemy property. Although contradictory stories are told about the eventual fate of the paintings, it seems that they were eventually restored to the Steins, who in turn sold them to Tetzen Lund, another early Matisse collector. Lund later sold them to Johannes Rump, a Danish engineer, who joined them to his own impressive collection, and eventually left them to the Statens Museum.

The Cone sisters were a different breed from the other important Matisse collectors. The sisters were perhaps the first outstanding examples of a twentieth-century type of collector which might be termed "the little collector." They were, in a sense, the forerunners of today's collector of modest means who buys the work of living artists, one or two paintings or drawings at a time, and happily hangs them with other cherished originals. Although the Cone sisters became well-to-do, they never lost the original attitude they had developed toward collecting when they first traveled abroad in 1901 with $2400 incomes.

Leo Stein pointed out that when he bought his first oil painting in 1902 he felt like a desperado, because art collecting in those days was something done only by the rich. The Cone sisters began by buying drawings from Picasso for two dollars apiece. With the same care and thoughtful discussion and attention to her pocketbook, Claribel bought *Mont Ste. Victoire* twenty-one years later for $18,000. It is the top price either of the sisters ever paid for one painting. Etta paid $15,000 for her Gauguin oil, *Woman with Mango*. That is the highest she ever went on a painting. A few other works, such as the Corot, *In the Studio,* were priced close to the limit Etta was willing to pay. Many of the sisters' paintings were bought for $500 to $600. A fair number bought in the late 1920s and in the 1930s cost a few thousand dollars. Morgan and Frick and other men of that stamp considered a half million dollars a little high for a painting, but not too high for a picture they coveted.

The personal relationship with Matisse always meant a great deal to Etta, somewhat less to Claribel. It is clear that the women would never have bought forty-three paintings by a dead artist. Knowing Matisse and admiring him definitely added to the pleasure of each purchase. The big collectors usually were not interested in an artist until he had been dead a few hundred years and had mellowed into an "old master." These millionaires had no desire for contact with living artists.

The fact that the collection was put together in such a personal and modest fashion gives the sisters an advantage over the "big" American collectors. The sisters had no Duveen, who advised Mr. Mellon, Mr. Morgan, and Mr. Huntington exactly which paintings to buy and which to by-pass. They had no Bernard Berenson, advising and scouting for an eager patroness, Isabella Stewart Gardner. They were unlike William Randolph Hearst, who bought millions of dollars' worth of art he had never seen, then shipped it to warehouses.

When the Cone sisters bought, after World War I, they bought for themselves; they bought by themselves. No dealer or art expert was consulted; none was needed. If any major art collection can be pointed to as a direct reflection of the personality of its creators this is the one. The color, the warmth, the gentleness of the majority of the paintings echo the mystique of the sisters. It is a harmonious whole. No impersonal note, added by another merely to dazzle and impress the spectator, spoils the unity. Those few which are notably bold, *The Blue Nude* and *The White Turban,* are accurate reflections of Claribel Cone's personality.

Do the sisters fairly belong in the ranks of that bold, original groups of collectors, Leo and Gertrude, Michael

and Sarah Stein, who seriously began buying important
Picasso and Matisse paintings in 1905 and 1906? The answer is simple; the Cone sisters do not belong to that
brave breed. They were witnesses to what we now regard
as historic moments, they were friends of the discoverers,
they were interested and sympathetic from the beginning, but they were not discoverers or pioneers. It took
almost a full generation before the sisters could bring
themselves to buy Matisse freely. Before World War I
they collected all sorts of decorative arts, as well as a few
paintings, sculptures, and drawings which the Steins
encouraged them to buy during their stays in Paris. It
wasn't until 1922 that the sisters bought without advice
and without encouragement from outside sources.

Their slow development as art collectors fits in with
another characteristic—their modest willingness to be
students all their lives. Claribel, in spite of her imposing
appearance, gave sure evidence of this trait in her medical career. She worked as a research student in the laboratory of Dr. William Welch, as well as at the Senckenberg Institute, until she was forty-six years old. Claribel
continued her various studies all her life, copying notes
into her little notebooks from the texts of others. Even
when she was a well-known art collector in Baltimore her
speeches on art were collections of quotations. She
studied languages intermittently all her life. Etta was an
indefatigable piano student even when she was well into
her seventies. The sisters were content, in 1925, to take
their notebooks to the classroom at Johns Hopkins University where Dr. George Boas was giving a course in

aesthetics. Perhaps because they both lacked a formal liberal arts education, the sisters never ceased to be intellectually eager and open. Fortunately, they trusted their intuition and taste in buying art to the same degree that they mistrusted offering their ideas to others.

What of the museum to which the sisters gave the sum of their lives? A museum is finally as good as its collections and Baltimore has been fortunate in producing spirited and active collectors who have, over the past thirty years, contributed generously to the museum.

. After the first galleries of the Baltimore Museum opened on Mount Vernon Place in 1923, plans were formulated to build a fireproof building to house the growing collections. Six years later the museum, designed in an innocuous style acceptable for public buildings in the 1920s, had a permanent home. The museum is situated on a rise at the edge of Wyman Park, neighboring the Johns Hopkins University. The solid, gray concrete, pillared building is reached by a long flight of steps flanked by two stone lions. Its impersonal façade features two large niches for sculpture; both are empty. A six-foot statue, an original of Rodin's *Thinker*, greenly weatherstained, sits on its pedestal at the top of the stairs.

The large, high-ceilinged entry hall seems like an architectural hangover from the days when an impressive entrance was considered as important as exhibition space. The galleries as they are presently used suggest two museum traditions. One is of the order that gives the donor a say in the setting for his art treasures. Hence the Baltimore Museum has a fair number of "period" rooms devoted to furniture and silver made by early Maryland craftsmen, as well as paintings by early Maryland artists. A collection of paintings of horses and horse racing, as well as trophies, is displayed in a room done in rich oak paneling, reminiscent of the den of an English country gentleman.

Galleries opposite the period rooms have been furbished recently with movable partitions, which offer the impersonal white-walled background considered necessary to an effective hanging of twentieth-century art. Passing through the museum's central hall, the visitor enters a glass-walled area surrounding an interior garden. The glass walls now serve the function of providing daylight for the hundreds of green plants massed near the wall. It is a pleasant rest for the eye. Opposite the greenery, display cases house sundry small objets d'art. Mounted on the walls above the cases are mosaics of the Antioch Expedition.

Two collections, donated by Jacob Epstein and Mary Frick Jacobs, provide the museum with "old master" galleries. Jacob Epstein, who bequeathed the museum its Rodin statue, also gave a fine painting by Van Dyck, *Rinaldo and Armida,* a *Portrait of a Bearded Man* by Titian, a *Portrait of a Young Man* by Frans Hals. Mr. Epstein lent his collections of old masters in 1929 when the museum, according to Mrs. Breeskin, "could call only a very few miscellaneous objects its own." The Epstein collection was bequeathed in 1946. The Mary Frick Jacobs collection, covering European painting from the fifteenth to the eighteenth centuries, includes Rembrandt's portrait of his son Titus, and a Frans Hals *Portrait of Dorothea Berck*. There are also eighteenth-century tapestries, furniture, and objets d'art. That collection was installed in 1937. The T. Harrison Garrett Collection of graphic art contains approximately 28,000 prints ranging from the fifteenth through the nineteenth centuries, with emphasis on Schongauer, Dürer, and Rembrandt. Two other Baltimore sisters, Blanche Adler and Saidie A. May, have been generous donors to the museum. The Blanche Adler collection features graphic arts of the late nineteenth and twentieth centuries. The Saidie A. May collection provides an interesting grouping of twentieth-century paintings, predominantly from the School of Paris. Those presented by Edward Joseph Gallagher give the viewer a survey of paintings by American artists created between 1921 and the present.

In the years following Etta Cone's death, prices on building materials rose so rapidly that her $400,000 bequest was found insufficient to build a new wing. Early in 1953 Philip Perlman asked the Board of Estimate of the City of Baltimore for $175,000. The initial request was denied because the board had already allocated its contingency fund for 1953. In May 1953 Perlman repeated his request, and the Board of Estimate agreed to provide the necessary funds from its 1954 budget. The bid accepted to build the wing came to $516,000. The museum was later allocated $11,000 to decorate the interior of the new wing.

There was no discussion on the part of the municipal

authorities on whether taxpayers' money should be spent to house modern art. The mayor, Walter d'Alesandro, was delighted with Baltimore's new treasure trove. When a visiting journalist suggested that the pictures were too good for Baltimore, he was reproved by the mayor. "Modern art," so long vilified, was now acceptable enough to enlist municipal support in its behalf. The "crazy" Matisses and Picassos were no longer considered crazy, and even if some still considered them so, they had become much too valuable to ignore. It must have been a source of quiet satisfaction to Etta Cone to know, in her last years, that her paintings, which her brothers had joked about, had indeed proved to be the "better investment" she had once predicted they would be.

The five galleries housing the paintings and sculpture of the Cone collection were opened to the public late in 1955. The galleries invite the visitor with a feeling of light, spaciousness, and a few unobtrusive furnishings. Nothing detracts from the importance of the paintings and sculpture. The cork tile floors muffle the spectator's footstep, the white walls give the paintings room at last to breathe and expand. The modern leather and chrome chairs and bench invite the visitors to sit before *The Blue Nude* or *The Magnolia Branch* for the minutes necessary to enjoy those works to the full. The lighting, recessed behind ceiling grids, is pleasantly bright and diffused, and there is no glare of light on glass, so annoying to the viewer in other museums. Large windows at one end of the galleries, curtained in a white, diaphanous fabric, add dimension and a desirable amount of daylight to the galleries. The main gallery is adjoined by two galleries to the left, two to the right.

The museum is a three-story building. The floor reached by the main entrance is actually the second floor; the ground floor houses the museum's library, a restaurant staffed by volunteers, the offices of the museum staff, storage rooms, the Wurtzberger collection of pre-Columbian art, and a changing exhibition of drawings and graphics lining the long halls.

On the third floor, above the Cone painting and sculpture galleries, is the new decorative arts section of the museum. Classrooms are also on this floor. A few pieces of the Cone furniture will be found gracing the decorative arts gallery; some are in the storerooms behind. At this writing the third floor of the museum is open to the public; during the winter months it contains examples of the laces, fabrics, and jewels from the Cone collection, as well as decorative arts given the museum by other donors. Behind the decorative arts gallery in the large storeroom one can see lying on steel shelving, wrapped in transparent plastic, the tapestries, the embroidered shawls, the priests' robes, the Kashmir shawls. Various pieces of furniture of the Cones and others stand disconsolately, deprived of their function in a home and not deemed worthy of museum exhibition. In a nearby room-sized vault a curator keeps the carefully catalogued jewel collection: Etta's twenty or thirty necklaces of coral; the elaborate necklace, bracelet, earring ensembles Claribel delighted to wear with her many shawls. Claribel's richly polished alligator jewel case, about twenty inches long, elaborately compartmented and velvet-lined, rests on a shelf.

Unhappily, the appearance of the Cone galleries and the installation of its works of art have been the cause of a considerable amount of quiet bitterness between the Cone family and the staff of the Baltimore museum. Etta Cone's will specifically bequeathed to the museum all of her collections the museum felt suitable for exhibition. Although Etta Cone did not stipulate what kind of wing she expected her $400,000 to build, the family and the museum have disagreed over the interpretation of an "appropriate" installation. Members of the family say firmly that Etta wished all of her paintings, sculpture, lace, fabrics, and jewelry to be shown together. Others say that Etta wanted her collections to be shown just as she had arranged them in her apartments; they believe Etta wanted a replica of her apartment built in the museum.

Mrs. Breeskin stated simply that Etta Cone did not like to talk about death and did not wish to discuss anything specific about the details of the installation. Her concern, Mrs. Breeskin felt, was to buy those paintings that would fill in the gaps in a collection that had become a historical survey of French painting from the middle of the nineteenth century to the middle of the twentieth. Before her death Etta Cone spoke worriedly to her friends about her ability to keep her estate intact so that she would be able to leave the museum enough money to build the wing. This concern was not realistic, since she left a substantial estate, but is indicative of the modesty of Etta Cone's attitudes.

No one will ever know exactly how Etta wished the Cone wing to look. No one living can say emphatically that she would have been pleased or displeased with the modern, unadorned wing that finally greeted the public. Her niece, Ellen Berney Hirschland, who traveled to Baltimore to be present at a gala evening opening, said of the galleries, "I looked all around trying to find something that reminded me of Aunt Etta. The only thing that did was an arrangement of dozens of red and violet anemone plants." Etta loved anemones; so did Matisse, who painted them many times.

Etta Cone's niece was one of many who felt that the apartments at the Marlborough were endowed with a unique charm. Some have said that the paintings never again seemed as bright or as rich in color once they were removed from the Cone apartments.

Perhaps because our country is still relatively young, there seems to be an unusually strong nostalgia in America for restoring or recreating historically important rooms and buildings. Having so much history and so many landmarks, the French are casual about marking sites that apply to twentieth-century history. The only plaques in Paris that remind the viewer of recent events are those placed in walls of buildings to show where members of the French Resistance fell in street battles with the Germans during World War II.

Certainly the French are not yet particularly concerned

about calling attention to the landmarks of twentieth-century art. When the author walked into the courtyard at 27 Rue de Fleurus on a May morning in 1960, there was no visible evidence that here stood a studio that had been inhabited by two of the discoverers of modern art. The Steins have vanished from 27 Rue de Fleurus as surely as if they had never been. The passageway Gertrude constructed in the 1920s to connect the atelier with the sleeping quarters is the only noticeable addition she made to the faded French courtyard. Otherwise the studio at 27 Rue de Fleurus is probably much the same as it was before Leo and Gertrude Stein moved there in 1903.

The same is true of the Rue Ravignan studio of Picasso, where Gertrude sat for her portrait. There are no plaques to mark the departed. Other artists live there now, courteous to the infrequent stranger who asks if this is the building where Picasso lived in 1905. Yes, it is, they answer, smiling, and return to their own painting. The little square of Place Emile Goudeau, with the softly spilling fountain, sits unchanged and unaffected by artists, past or present.

The case is different with the apartment at 5 Rue Christine where Gertrude Stein lived in Paris until her death in 1946. In the spring of 1960 Miss Toklas still lived there; many of the Picasso and Gris paintings were hanging. Among them was the first Picasso bought by Leo, *Girl with a Bouquet,* which Gertrude found so distressing. Next to the mantel in the living room, near the chair where Miss Toklas sat to read and answer her large correspondence, hung four or five small oil sketches by Picasso of African heads; these were preliminary sketches for *Les Demoiselles d'Avignon*. Gertrude Stein willed her portrait by Picasso to the Metropolitan Museum; the other paintings will remain with Miss Toklas during her lifetime; then pass to Allan Stein's three children.

What of the collection of Michael and Sarah Stein? The building at 58 Rue Madame is now a boys' school. Photos of their house, Les Terrasses, at Garches, designed by Le Corbusier, have found their way into anthologies on modern architecture, and the house has become a classic. After the death of Michael Stein in Palo Alto in 1938, Sarah stayed on there. She graciously greeted a new generation who found their way to her door, come to see her paintings. Sarah, of whom Matisse once said, "She knows more about my paintings than I do," enjoyed showing her collection and telling her stories. She outlived all of the other Steins and the Cone sisters. Her last years were spent in a cloudy senility, during which she was persuaded to sell many of her paintings to unscrupulous dealers at ridiculous prices. Her close friend, Mrs. Walter Haas, bought *Femme au Chapeau* at a fair price. She tried to persuade Sarah to sell paintings, if she must, only to trusted friends. Sarah was interested only in raising money for her grandson and was too removed from reality to heed the advice of Mrs. Haas. By the time of her death in 1953 the collection, which she had intended to give to Stanford University, was almost totally dissipated. Friends have subsequently bought Henri Matisse's portraits of Michael and Sarah Stein and given them to the San Francisco Museum, hoping others would come forth to donate paintings once owned by the Steins, and assist in reassembling for the public what was once a great collection. Leo Stein's collection had been sold long before his death in 1947.

Henri Matisse outlived them all. He was productive to the day of his death, although a semi-invalid for the last fifteen years of his life. It was said by *Life* magazine that Matisse spent his last morning, November 3, 1954, working on a large new decoration. He sat quietly, directing an assistant where to place the miraculously designed paper shapes he had begun cutting in the years after he could no longer hold a brush. Matisse's daughter Margot and his secretary-model, Lydia Delectorskaya, were at his bedside when he died that night.

"Two Women"

by Gertrude Stein

THERE ARE OFTEN two of them, both women. There were two of them, two women. There were two of them, both women. There were two of them. They were both women. There were two women and they were sisters. They both went on living. They were very often together then when they were living. They were very often not together when they were living. One was the elder and one was the younger. They always knew this thing, they always knew that one was the elder and one was the younger. They were both living and they both went on living. They were together and they were then both living. They were then both going on living. They were not together and they were both living then and they both went on living then. They sometimes were together, they sometimes were not together. One was older and one was younger.

When they were together they said to each other that they were together and that each one of them was being living then and was going on then being living. When they were together they called each other sister. When they were together they knew they were together. When they were together, they were together and they were not changing then, they were together then.

There were two of them, they were both women, they were sisters, they were together and they were being living then and they were going on being living then and they were knowing then that they were together. They were not together and they were living then and they were each of them going on being living then and they were knowing then that they were not together.

Each of them were being living. Each of them were going on being living. Each of them was one of the two of them. One of them was older. One of them was younger. They were sometimes together. They were sometimes not together. The younger called the older sister Martha. The older called the younger Ada. They each one knew that the other one needed being one being living. They each one knew that the other one was going on being living. They each one knew that that one needed to be one being living. They each one knew that that one was going on being living. The younger knew that the older was going on being living. The older did not know that the younger was going on being living.

The older knew that the younger would be going on living. They both were going on being living. They were both needing being one being living.

They were together and they spoke of each other as their sister. Each one was certain that the other one was a sister. They were together and they were both then being living. The younger one called the older sister Martha. The older called the younger Ada. They were together and they were then both of them going on being living.

The older one was more something than the younger one. The younger one was not so much something as the older one. The older one was more something than the younger one. The younger one was receiving everything in being one going on being living. The older one was more something than the younger one. The older one was going on being living, the older one was telling about this thing about being more something than the younger one. The older one was telling about this thing about the younger one being more something than any other one. The younger one was telling about being more something than any other one. The younger one was not telling about the older one being more something than any other one. The younger one was telling about both of them being more something than any other one.

They were together and they knew it then, knew that they were together. They were not together and they knew it then, knew that they were not together. They both went on being living. Later they were not together.

They knew it then both of them that they were not then together. Later then they were together. They knew it then, both of them, that they were then together.

They did some things. The elder did some things. The older one went on being living. She did some things. She went on being living. She did this thing, she went on being living. She did some things. She did go on being living. She was more something than any other one. She did some things. She went on being living. She did this thing, she went on being living.

The younger one did some things. She was receiving some things more than any other one. She went on receiving them. She went on being living. She received this thing, she went on being living. She had this thing more than any other one, receiving going on being living. She received this thing, she went on being living. She received going on being living. She received this more than any other one. She went on being living. She was receiving this thing, she was receiving it more than any other one. She was receiving it some from her sister Martha she received it more from every one. She received this thing, she received going on being living.

They were together and they knew that then, the two of them, both of them knew it then, knew that they were together. They were not together and they knew it then, both of them knew it then, each one of the two of them knew it then, knew that they were not together then.

There were others connected with them, connected with each of them, connected with both of them. There were some connected with both of them. There had been

a father and there had been a mother and there were
brothers and quite enough of them. They each of them
had certainly duties toward these connected with them.
They had, each one of them, what they wanted, Martha
when she wanted it, Ada when she was going to want it.
They had brothers and a mother and a father. They
were quite rich, all of them. They were sometimes together, the two of them, they were sometimes travelling.
They were sometimes alone together then. They knew it
then. They were sometimes not alone together then.
They knew that then. They were, the two of them, ones
travelling and they were then ones buying some things
and they were then ones living in a way and they were
then ones sometimes living in another way. They were
very different the one from the other of them. They
were certainly very different.

They each of them knew some who were knowing
them. They each of them pleased some who were knowing them. They each of them were pleased by some who
were knowing them. They were large women, both of
them, anybody could see them. They were large women
either of them. Very many saw them. Very many saw each
one of them. Some saw them. Really not very many saw
them, saw both of them. They were large women. Really
not very many saw both of them. And that was a natural
thing. There were two of them. They were together and
they knew it then. They were not together and they
knew it then. They were both large women and they
were very different the one from the other of them, very
different, and one, Ada, was younger and called her sister,

279

sister Martha, and one, Martha was older and called her
sister Ada.

There were two of them. They were each one of them
rich. They each one of them had what they wanted,
Martha when she was wanting, Ada when she was going
to be wanting. And they both had not what they were
wanting. The older Martha because she was not wanting
it and the younger Ada because she could not come to
want it. They both of them were spending money that
they had and they were both of them very different one
from the other of them. They were both of them doing
what they were doing that is to say Martha was doing
what she was doing that is to say she was not changing in
doing what she was doing, that is to say she was going on
and that was something that she was saying was a curious
thing, that she was doing what she was doing and not
changing and not doing that thing. Ada was doing what
she was doing that is to say she needed to be doing what
she was doing, that is to say she was having what she was
having to do and she was doing what she was doing, that
is to say she was doing what she was doing and any one
could be certain that she was doing what she would be
doing, that is to say she was doing what she would be
coming to be doing and certainly then sister Martha was
with her then and certainly then Ada was not doing that
thing, certainly then Ada was doing something, certainly
then she had something to do and certainly then she was
doing something and certainly then her sister Martha
was not then changing and certainly then they were rich
ones and buying things and living in a way and some-

times then they were living in another way and buying
some things and sometimes then they were not together
and then they did not know it then that they were not
any longer travelling together. They were each of them
rich then. There were some whom they pleased then,
each one of them, that is to say there were some who
knew each one of them, there were some who knew both
of them. There were two of them, they were sisters.
There was an older one and she pleased some and she
was interesting to some and some pleased her. There was
a younger one and she was pleasing some and she was
feeling something about this thing and feeling something about some pleasing her some. There were two of
them, they were sisters, they were large women, they were
rich, they were very different one from the other one,
they had brothers enough of them, the older one had
what she wanted when she wanted it, that is to say she
did not have what she wanted because she did not want it.
The younger had what she wanted when she was coming
to want it, that is to say she did not have what she wanted
as she could not come to want it. They were living together in a way and then they were living together in
another way and then they were not living together.

The older one was one who did with distinction telling about being one being living. She was one who was
being living. She was one telling about this thing and
many people were not listening. She was telling about
this thing about being one being living, telling about this
thing with some distinction and some were knowing this
thing were knowing that she was telling this thing, tell-

ing about being living and telling it with distinction and they were not listening, were not listening to her telling about this thing, telling about being living, telling with distinction about being living. She was one being living and she was telling about this thing telling about it very often, beginning and going on then and certainly very many then were not listening.

The younger one was one being living and she was telling about this thing, telling again and again about this thing about being living and she was telling this thing and some were listening, certainly some were listening, and she was telling again and again about being one being living and certainly some were listening and certainly she did this thing again and again, she told about being one being living and certainly anybody might not be going on being listening and certainly some were listening and certainly some went on listening. And certainly sometime not any one was really listening, certainly some time pretty nearly not any one was really listening and certainly sometime she was to herself not telling about this thing not telling about being living and certainly in a way she was always telling about this thing telling about being living and certainly then in a way the older one was listening, and certainly then in a way not any one was listening.

The older one went on living, the younger went on living, they both went on living. The older one went on living. Certainly she went on living and certainly some were enjoying this thing enjoying that she was going on living, some who were not then listening, some who certainly would not be listening and she certainly would be telling and telling with distinction of being one being living. Some were certainly enjoying this thing that she was one being living. Anybody could be pleasant with this thing that she was being living. Mostly every one could not be listening to her telling this thing telling of being one being living and certainly all of living in her was being one telling with distinction of being one being living. She was being living, any one could remember this thing, any one could be pleasant in this thing, some could be tired of this thing, not really tired of this thing, any one could be pleasant with this thing, some were very pleasant in this thing in her being one being living.

The younger one was one being living, any one could be tired of this thing of this one being one being living, any one could come to be tired of this thing of this one being one being living. Any one could be careful of this thing of this one going on being living, almost any one could be pretty careful of this thing of this one being one being living. This one was one being one being living. Very many were quite careful of this thing of this one being one being living.

These two were being ones who were being living. They had been for some time ones being living. They had been living each one of them, they were living, each one of them, they were going on living each one of them. They were, each one of them, being living, they had been being living, they were going on being living. Each of them was a different one from the other one in having been living, in being living, in going on being living.

The older was one and any one could know this thing for certainly if she was not such a one she was not anything and every one knew she was something, the older one was one who had distinction and certainly she said that she did not do anything to be any one and certainly she did everything and certainly not anything was anything and would not be anything if she were not one having distinction. And certainly she was one having distinction and certainly some were interested in this thing and certainly she was doing nothing and certainly she was doing everything and certainly very many were very tired of this thing of her not doing anything, of her doing something, and certainly any one could know she was a person of distinction. She certainly did not do anything, that is to say she certainly never had done anything. She certainly did anything, that is to say she certainly was always going on doing something. She told about such a thing, she told about going on doing something, she told about never having done anything. She certainly never had done anything. She certainly was always really going on doing something.

She was a person of some distinction. She was not ever changing in this thing. She was not ever changing in anything. She was not changing in being one being living. She was not changing in being one not having done anything. She was not changing in being one going on doing something. She was not changing about anything. She was not changing in telling about this thing. She was not changing and certainly any one could come to be certain of this thing. She was certain of this thing, any one could

be certain of this thing, any one could come to hear her
be certain of this thing. She was a person of distinction.
She was not changing in this thing. She had not ever done
anything. She was not changing in this thing. She was
going on in doing something. She was not changing in
this thing. She was needing that any one was knowing
any of these things. She was always needing this thing
needing that any one was knowing any of these things,
was knowing that she was not changing, that she had distinction, that she had not done anything, that she was
going on doing something. She was needing that any one
was knowing some of these things. Some were knowing
some of these things, she needed that thing. Certainly her
sister knew some of these things and certainly in a way
that was not any satisfaction, certainly that was in a way
considerable satisfaction, and certainly there was in a
way considerable satisfaction in their being two being
living who were, the one sister Martha and the other
Ada, considerable satisfaction to almost any one. They
talked to each other about some things, they did not talk
to each other about everything and certainly they both
were needing this thing that some one was knowing that
they were being ones being living and not being then two
of them, being then each of them.

The older, sister Martha, talked some and certainly
she wanted to hear talking, and certainly some do want
to talk some and want to hear talking and it is about
something, something which they have not ever been
doing and certainly some of such of them will not in any
way really be doing any such thing, not in any way really

be doing anything of any such thing. The older, sister Martha certainly was willing, was needing to be willing to be talking, to be listening to talking about something and certainly she would not ever in any way be doing anything of any such thing. Certainly she was one, if she had been one who was more of the kind she was in being living would have been needing to be really doing some such thing again and again. And certainly she was not ever really doing anything of any such thing and that was because she was one not needing to be willing to be doing any such thing and she was one needing to be telling and listening to telling about doing such a thing. Certainly she was one quite completely needing to be telling and to be listening to telling about doing some such thing. Certainly she was not one ever needing to be willing to be in any way doing any such thing. And this would be puzzling if it were not completely a certain thing and it is completely this thing. She was one being one of a kind of them that when they are that kind of them are ones completely needing to be doing some thing, some one thing. She was of that kind of them. She was of a kind of them and that kind of them when they are that kind of them are ones needing to be willing to be doing, really doing one thing and she was of that kind of them and she was not needing to be willing to be doing that thing. She was of a kind of them and some of that kind of them are ones needing to be telling and to be listening to telling about doing a thing and she was of that kind of them and more and more she was completely needing to be listening and to be telling and to be asking and to be answering about doing that thing. There are some and they are of this kind of them and they certainly are not telling or not talking about this thing, are not listening, are not asking, are not needing to be willing to be hearing, to be telling anything about any such a thing. Sister Martha then was of a kind of them of ones being existing.

Ada, the younger, certainly was of a kind of them of a kind being existing. She was one certainly having certainly talking, she and sister Martha certainly were listening and were talking and about something they certainly were needing to be willing to be talking about and listening about. Ada, the younger, was one not willing to be needing to be doing that thing and certainly she was completely needing doing that thing and certainly she was not ever completely needing to be willing to be doing that thing. And this then was soon not completely interesting to any one but her sister Martha who certainly was interested in any such thing.

Ada, the younger, was one being living and certainly she was one being living in needing anything that was in her being living to be being living. She certainly was using anything in being living. That is to say she needed to be one being living and certainly she was needing to be using anything that could be something being living for her to be one being living. That is she was one needing being one being living, that is she was one needing to be one going on being living. She certainly was needing this thing, needing being one going on being living, and she was one not easily feeding to be one going on being living. Feeding on being living to be one going on being living was a thing that she was not easily doing. She certainly was needing to be one going on being living. She certainly was not one easily being living to be one going on being living. She certainly was needing to be one going on being living. She certainly was not easily feeding on being living, on anything being living, she certainly was needing being one going on being living. She was feeding some on something being living, on some things being existing, on being living being existing and she was going on being living. She was needing going on being living. She did go on being living.

She was sometimes together with sister Martha, she was sometimes not together with her. She was one being living. She was needing going on being living. She was going on being living.

Any one being living can be one having been something. Not any one, some being living, can be one having been something. Some being living have been one being something. Certainly having been doing something and then not doing that thing and having been something and certainly then being something is something that has been making a living that is almost a family living in some one. Certainly sister Martha and Ada had been ones having family living and certainly they were ones having family living and certainly they were ones going to be having family living and certainly family living is something that is not existing in a family living together in any daily living. And certainly each one of them, each one of the two of them were living and had been living

and certainly very many were certain of this thing and
certainly such a family living was a thing to be remembering and certainly some could be certain that such a
family living made any one have a finer feeling, and
sometimes some one was quite certain that fine feeling
was not then existing and certainly this thing was interesting to sister Martha and not convincing and certainly this thing was not interesting to Ada and sister
Martha was not repeating this thing any too often and
Ada was quite certain of any such thing, of fine feeling
in a way being existing and sister Martha was pretty
nearly certain of some such thing.

They were both of them certain that there was some
connection between loving and listening between liking
and listening and certainly some listened to each one of
them and certainly there were some who were listening
and liking the one to whom they were listening and certainly there were some who were listening and some
having some tender feeling for the one to whom they
were listening.

The older one, sister Martha, was one in a way needing
that there should be some connection between liking and
listening between liking her and listening to her and she
was not in any way suffering in this thing, through this
thing, she was not suffering for certainly some were listening and really then listening being existing certainly
something was then being existing, listening was being
existing, and certainly in a way there being some connection between liking and listening something was certainly in a way being existing. The older one then was

one being living in something being existing and listening being existing, something was being existing, and there being some connection between liking and listening, certainly something was being existing.

The younger one was certain that there was completely a connection between tender feeling and listening, between liking and listening and she certainly was completely suffering in this thing, suffering from this thing. She was completely suffering and there certainly was connection between tender feeling and listening and liking and listening. She was almost completely suffering and certainly some were listening, quite a number were quite listening and certainly there is some connection between tender feeling and listening, and liking and listening. She had been suffering and she was suffering in there being a connection between tender feeling and listening, and between liking and listening. Quite a number were listening, certainly, quite a number were listening and in a way she was quite certain of this thing, quite certain that quite a number were listening and she was quite certain, she was completely certain that there was connection between listening and tender feeling, and listening and liking. She certainly had been, she certainly was going on suffering from this thing, she certainly was suffering in this thing. She was certain that some were listening and she went on being certain of this thing that quite a number were listening and certainly quite a number were listening to her and certainly that was going on being existing. She certainly was suffering in this thing in their being existing a connection between listening and liking and listening and tender feeling.

They were together and they were very often then not together. Certainly each one of them was sometimes then not with any other one. That is to say the older one was sometimes then not with any other one, she was very often not with any one and always then some one, some were in a way doing something and certainly then were meeting this one who was then being living. This one the older one in a way was very often not with any one. She was quite often not with any one. She certainly was not needing this thing. She certainly was not certain that she was not needing this thing. She was being living and certainly then very often she was not with any one.

She was not needing anything and she was needing being living and she was needing anything that she was needing for this thing for being living. She could be needing very much for this thing for being living. She was having something to be doing this thing to be being living, she was using a good deal for this thing for being living and in a way she was not needing anything and she was needing to be living and she was using quite enough for this thing for being living.

She was using some for this thing, for being living, that is to say if not any one were living she would not be living and really then she was not using them very much, she was not using any one very much, she was using them and really she was not needing that they should be any one. She was not using women and men and not at all children to be one being living. She was not using any one of any of them. She was needing being living and a good deal was being existing in this thing, she was not using very much of anything for this thing, a good deal had to be existing for this thing.

She was very often not with any one, quite often not with any one and she was being living and enough had to be being existing for this thing, quite a good deal had to be existing for this thing. She was one not needing to be very often with not any one. She was one not needing anything, not needing any one, she was one needing, pretty well needing being living and she was one needing that enough things be existing and in a way she was not using any of them anything being existing.

The younger one was sometimes not with any one and certainly this was not what this one was needing she certainly was needing being with some one and certainly she was sometimes with her sister Martha and in a way she was not ever really needing this thing needing being with the older one. She certainly was needing that the older one, that sister Martha had been and was being existing. She the younger one was certainly needing using something and some one and very often any one and certainly very often she was not doing this thing she was not using anything she was not using any one and certainly then she was with some one for she was one who certainly was needing going on being living. She certainly was needing that she was going on being living and certainly she was completely needing for this thing to be using some to be using some things and certainly sometimes she was almost completely not using anything not using any one and certainly then she was still with some one, still with something for certainly she was one going on being living.

Certainly each one of them were ones that might have been better looking, might have been very good-looking when they were younger ones and this had not been, they had not been as good-looking when they were younger ones as they were when they were older ones neither the one nor the other of them. They were quite good-looking when they were older ones, they were quite big enough then for this thing for being good-looking and quite old enough then for being good-looking, they were big then and old enough then and they certainly were quite good-looking then. When they were older ones they were ones saying again and again and again, and some one always was listening, what they had had as pretty nearly feeling when they were younger ones. When they were younger ones they certainly were feeling some thing and certainly then they were not ever completely saying that thing saying what they were feeling and they were certainly not then saying it again and again and they certainly were then not completely feeling that thing the thing they were later in being older ones saying completely and again and again and again. They were, each one of them, saying something when they were young ones and saying it again and again and they were feeling that thing and they were really feeling something and more and more they were ones completely feeling that thing and completely saying it again and again and again and again and again. They were, each one of them completely feeling a different thing from the other one of them and completely saying that completely different thing. Each one of them was completely saying a complete thing and saying it again and again and again and again and again and again and again .

Martha was quite young once and that was never of any interest to herself or any one. She did some things then, that was a natural thing. She was not ever completely interested in having done any of them. She was quite young then a completely young one and not any one then was very proud of this thing that she was a young one then. Some one may have been then a little proud of this thing that she was a young one then, it was not an interesting thing her being, her having been a young one.

She had been a quite young one, there were many others in the family then, some being very young ones then some being a little older ones then, there were always many others in the family and that was certainly a thing that was quite interesting.

Martha then was not any longer such a quite young one. She certainly then was doing something. Any one could then have been proud of that thing that she was certainly then doing something. Enough were then proud of that thing that she was doing something. She was interested enough in that thing that she was doing something. All her life then, all the rest of her living, she was doing that thing she was interested enough in doing that thing, some were proud enough of that thing that she was doing that thing. And certainly she was interested enough in doing that thing and certainly what she had done and was doing was not in any way completely interesting and it was almost completely interesting as being something that she had been all her living doing and finding interesting to be one being doing that thing. So then Martha was not any longer quite a young one and certainly then there were a good many of them and they were all of them being ones any one could be remembering as being in the family living. There were many of them and all of them were proud enough and interested enough in this thing and certainly Martha was one of them and certainly not any one of them was completely anything excepting that any one of them and all of them were being living.

Martha was then one being living. She was then not such a young one, she was almost then an older one and certainly then she was being living and so were all of them and so was any one of them. Certainly any one of them might have it come that something would stop in going on and then that one would not be any longer living. Certainly this could certainly this did happen to some of them and certainly then all of them were remembering this thing that something could be stopping in them and they would then not be being living. And this could sometime happen to Martha and she could sometimes be remembering to think about this thing and this then was not an interesting thing as happening to any one of them, it was an interesting thing as being something happening to each of them and certainly it was not a thing going to happen to each of them but it was as such an interesting thing to Martha and as such she was completely remembering it and certainly she was almost remembering that perhaps it would not be happening to herself ever and certainly it could be happening to herself.

Ada the younger one was always completely remembering such a thing could be happening to herself, she was always completely remembering this thing. She was always completely remembering that there were very many of them. She was not always completely remembering that this thing could be happening to every one of them. She was very often remembering this thing that that could be happening to all of them, she was always completely remembering that it could be happening to herself, she was not ever completely remembering that that thing could be happening to any one of them, she was remembering this thing after it had happened to one of them and she was completely remembering this thing after it had happened to another one of them, and she completely remembered this thing after it had happened to another one of them. Certainly this thing did not happen to her in her being living and certainly she completely remembered all her being living that it would happen to her in her being living.

She had been a young one a quite young one and this had been completely enough interesting to her then so that she was completely certain that having been a quite young one was a thing that any one could be remembering. She had been a completely young one and certainly then she had been then not doing anything and certainly she completely remembered this thing and some other ones could remember this thing. Even her sister Martha could remember this thing and certainly she did not remember this thing. Certainly some did remember this thing. Ada was then not such a quite young one and certainly then she did not do anything and certainly then it was an important thing to any of them that she was then being one who was one remembering that each one was being living then and needing this thing needing being living. She was one then who was not completely interested in that thing in herself then, in being one being living, she was certainly then being completely interested in being one going on being living. She always went on being living.

Surely Ada would like to have been one going on living and she was remembering that she had been going on living and she was remembering that she had been liking going to be enjoying something then. She certainly, then when she had been going on being living, she had been certain that she could be coming to be enjoying something that sometime she would be having. She certainly was needing then to be going to be enjoying something. She certainly was then going to be enjoying some one and she certainly knew this thing then and could tell any one this thing then that she would be enjoying some one and certainly then she was going on being living.

She certainly could remember this thing, in a way she could remember anything, and certainly in a way she did remember everything. She always could remember that she would enjoy some, that she would enjoy somethings. She always did remember that she had been going on being living. She always could remember this thing. She always did remember this thing. She always could remember that she would enjoy some, that she could enjoy some things, that she needed this thing to be one going on being living and she always could remember that she had always been going on being living. She could remember everything. She was remembering everything. She was remembering that she had been going on being living. She remembered that she could enjoy some, that she could enjoy somethings, that she had needed this to be one going on being living. She could remember everything. She did remember everything. She remembered again and again that she had gone on being living. She remembered again and again that she could remember this thing that she could remember, that she did remember that she had gone on being living. She did remember this thing. She remembered some other things. She remembered everything. She remembered that anything might happen and that certainly she was not needing that thing that anything was happening. She remembered and remembered and remembered it again and again that not any one was remembering any such thing that anything might be happening and that she was completely remembering this thing. She remembered this thing and she remembered that she had been going on being living.

She was not, to every one, remembering everything, and certainly she did remember this thing, she did remember that, to some, she did not remember everything, she did remember that some did not remember everything, that they did not remember that she could remember everything. She could certainly not forget this thing that some did not remember everything.

She certainly was one needing going on being living. She certainly was being living. She certainly had been going on being living. She certainly was going on being living. She certainly went on being living. She certainly remembered everything of this thing of going on being living. She certainly remembered everything. She certainly remembered about some remembering everything. She certainly remembered about some not remembering anything. She certainly could remember everything. She certainly remembered again and again this thing remembered that she could remember everything.

She was younger than her sister. Her sister was older. She called her sister, sister Martha, her sister called her Ada. When they were together they were each one of them certainly being living, the older was then certainly being living, she was knowing that thing, her sister was knowing that thing, the younger was then going on being living, the younger then knew that thing, the older one then knew that thing.

They were together and they were both being living then. They were not together and they were both being living then. The older was being living then. The younger was going on being living then.

The younger one was always remembering that they were both being living. The older was not ever forgetting that they were both being living. The younger was knowing that the older was being living, was knowing that she herself was needing going on being living. The older was knowing that the younger was going on being living, that she was needing this thing, she was knowing that she herself was being living.

Etta Cone's Will

Portion of Last Will and Testament of Etta Cone refer-
ring to her art collection; dated May 18, 1949

I, ETTA CONE, of Baltimore, Maryland, do make, pub-
lish and declare this my Last Will and Testament, as follows, that is to say:

FIRST: I hereby revoke, cancel and annul any and all
former Wills and Codicils at any time heretofore made
by me.

SECOND: I direct that all my just debts and funeral expenses first be paid.

THIRD: Whereas by her Last Will and Testament
dated the twenty-fifth day of April, 1929, my late sister,
Dr. Claribel Cone, of Baltimore, Maryland, bequeathed
to me for the term of my natural life, her Art Collection,
more particularly mentioned and described in the Paragraph numbered Thirteenth in said Last Will and Testament, and further gave and bequeathed to me a full and
unrestricted power of appointment to name, appoint and
designate such person or persons, institution or institutions, as I may elect to take and receive the said Art Col-

lection at and after my death: Now, therefore, in exercise of and pursuant to the said power of appointment, I do hereby name, appoint, designate and elect the BALTIMORE MUSEUM OF ART, INCORPORATED, and the MAYOR AND CITY COUNCIL OF BALTIMORE, to take, have and receive the aforesaid Art Collection at and after my death, and I hereby give, grant and bequeath to said BALTIMORE MUSEUM OF ART, INCORPORATED, and the MAYOR AND CITY COUNCIL OF BALTIMORE the said Art Collection and all right, title and interest therein which I am authorized, empowered or have the right to dispose of.

FOURTH: And whereas in the paragraph numbered Fourteenth of her said Last Will and Testament, my said sister, Dr. Claribel Cone, of Baltimore, Maryland, directed that the sum of One Hundred Thousand Dollars ($100,000.00) be set apart and separately invested and all of the rents, issues, income and profit therefrom be paid to me so long as I shall live and on my death that the said principal sum of One Hundred Thousand Dollars ($100,000.00) shall be added to and become a part of said Art Collection, and shall be subject to the power of appointment conferred upon me: Now, therefore, in exercise of and pursuant to the said power of appointment, I do hereby name, appoint, designate and elect the said BALTIMORE MUSEUM OF ART, INCORPORATED, and the MAYOR AND CITY COUNCIL OF BALTIMORE to take and receive said principal sum of One Hundred Thousand Dollars ($100,000.00) at and after my death, provided, however, that the said principal sum of One Hundred

Thousand Dollars ($100,000.00) and the income there-from shall be expended by the said Baltimore Museum of Art, Incorporated, and the said Mayor and City Council of Baltimore for the purpose of housing, preserving, maintaining and caring for the aforesaid Art Collection, or for the purpose of improving or adding thereto, as stipulated and provided in the said Last Will and Testament of my said sister, Dr. Claribel Cone. And I hereby give and bequeath to said BALTIMORE MUSEUM OF ART, INCORPORATED, and the MAYOR AND CITY COUNCIL OF BALTIMORE, in so far as I am authorized and empowered so to do, the said sum of One Hundred Thousand Dollars ($100,000.00) so set apart by my said sister, Dr. Claribel Cone, for the uses and purposes aforesaid, and all right, title and interest therein which I am authorized, empowered or have the right to dispose of. Notwithstanding the authority contained in the Last Will and Testament of my said sister, Dr. Claribel Cone, I do not desire that any part of this bequest shall be used for the purpose of improving or adding to the Art Collection, but that all of it be used for the other purposes specified in said Last Will and Testament.

FIFTH: And whereas in addition to the aforesaid Art Collection of my said sister, Dr. Claribel Cone, I have accumulated, own and possess another Art Collection hereinafter designated as my Personal Art Collection, both the said Art Collections being collections largely of Modern Art, and being in large part supplementary to each other; and whereas it was always the desire and intention of both my said sister, Dr. Claribel Cone, and myself, that eventually the two collections be merged and formed into one larger collection, now, therefore, in order to consummate the said purpose: In addition to the appointment of said BALTIMORE MUSEUM OF ART, INCORPORATED, and the MAYOR AND CITY COUNCIL OF BALTIMORE to receive said Art Collection of my sister, Dr. Claribel Cone, as provided in the foregoing Third Paragraph of this, my Last Will and Testament, I do also give, devise and bequeath, with the exceptions hereinafter noted, to said BALTIMORE MUSEUM OF ART, INCORPORATED, and the MAYOR AND CITY COUNCIL OF BALTIMORE, my said Personal Art Collection now owned by me or which I may hereafter acquire, the same consisting of sundry pictures, oil paintings, water colors, lithographs, colored aquatints, etchings, prints, drawings, engravings, photographs, whether the same be framed or unframed; also all of my laces, jewelry, shawls, fabrics, rugs, draperies, portieres, embroideries and other textiles, bric-a-brac, bronzes, antique furniture, marbles, sculptures, curios and other objets d'art which form part of my said Personal Art Collection; and also all of my art library, including all of the books, catalogues, pamphlets, periodicals and other publications. It is my desire that this bequest shall not include any duplicates of books, bronzes, prints, lithographs and other art objects, and shall not include anything lacking in museum value or interest. I hereby nominate and appoint a committee, consisting of the President of the Board of Trustees of the Baltimore Museum of Art, the Director of said Museum, my sister-in-law, Laura W. Cone, Greensboro, North Carolina, and my friends, David Rosen, technical adviser of the Walters Art Gallery, Baltimore, Maryland, and Philip B. Perlman, member of the boards of trustees of the Baltimore Museum of Art and the Walters Art Gallery, to determine which items shall be included in this bequest and which are to be excluded as duplicates, or as lacking museum value or interest. In the event that any members of the committee named by me herein shall decline to serve, or shall resign or (in the case of any of the individuals specifically named) shall not be living at the time of my death or shall die before the task is completed, then I hereby authorize a majority of those remaining to fill any vacancies. The determinations by the committee shall be final and binding upon all parties in interest.

All expenses incurred by the committee, including the employment of assistants or experts, shall be paid by my Executors out of the rest, residue and remainder of my estate.

I hereby give and bequeath all items designated by the committee as duplicates to the WOMEN'S COLLEGE OF THE UNIVERSITY OF NORTH CAROLINA, for use in its Art Department and in the Weatherspoon Art Gallery of said college and university.

SIXTH: In addition to the foregoing, and subject to the provisions of the Paragraph hereinafter numbered Seventh of this my Last Will and Testament, I give and be-

queath to the said BALTIMORE MUSEUM OF ART, INCOR-
PORATED, and the MAYOR AND CITY COUNCIL OF BALTI-
MORE, out of my own personal estate (and additional to
the fund referred to in the Fourth Paragraph hereof) the
further sum of Three Hundred Thousand Dollars
($300,000.00) to be used for the purpose of erecting and
equipping a building, wing or addition to the Baltimore
Museum of Art to house and contain the two aforesaid
Art Collections bequeathed by my sister, Dr. Claribel
Cone, and by myself. The two cash bequests to the said
BALTIMORE MUSEUM OF ART, INCORPORATED, and the
MAYOR AND CITY COUNCIL OF BALTIMORE under the provisions of this and the preceding Fourth Paragraph of
this Will total the sum of Four Hundred Thousand Dollars ($400,000.00) toward the cost of erecting and equip-
ping a building, wing or addition to the building occupied by the Baltimore Museum of Art, and to preserve
and maintain and care for said Art Collections.

I make the bequests of art collections and fund jointly
to the Baltimore Museum of Art, Incorporated, and the
Mayor and City Council of Baltimore because the title
to the land and buildings occupied by the Museum is in
the Mayor and City Council of Baltimore, and any new
building will belong to the city. I desire that the city and
the Museum cooperate in making the expenditures required by the additional construction, and that the building and other contracts be awarded by the city in the
manner provided in the Baltimore City Charter. Inas-
much as, under existing conditions, there may be some
delay before the building or wing can be constructed, I

direct that, in the event any delay is inevitable, the fund paid over to the Museum and the city by my executors shall be invested, and the income therefrom added to principal and used for the purposes of the bequests. In the event that the bequests are insufficient for the purposes, I request that the Mayor and City Council of Baltimore provide such additional amounts as may be necessary; and, in the event that a building or wing is constructed and equipped within the amounts provided by me then I direct that any excess be used, in the discretion of the Trustees of the Baltimore Museum of Art, Incorporated, for the maintenance and preservation of the collections.

SEVENTH: It is my desire and request that the two Art Collections hereinabove bequeathed in the Paragraphs numbered Third and Fifth hereof be merged or kept together, housed and maintained as a unit collection, and that the same be known as "THE CONE COLLECTION, FORMED BY DR. CLARIBEL CONE AND MISS ETTA CONE OF BALTIMORE, MARYLAND." I desire that such paintings, textiles and other objects of art as were bequeathed to the Baltimore Museum of Art, Incorporated, by my brother, the late Frederic W. Cone, be kept together with the Cone Collection, and that they be labeled or marked with his name. I direct that the Baltimore Museum of Art, Incorporated, and the Mayor and City Council of Baltimore, as a condition to the bequests made in the Paragraphs numbered Third, Fourth, Fifth and Sixth hereof, agree that they will not sell or dispose of any of the items forming part of the Cone Collection, but that it shall be kept permanently as received, without addition and without elimination.

EIGHTH: It is my will and intention that my Executors shall not be in any way responsible for the preservation or safe-keeping of either of the aforesaid Art Collections, but the same shall at all times be at the entire risk of the eventual beneficiary thereof. My Executors shall not be required, unless in their discretion they deem fit to do so, and then only to such extent as they may see fit, to insure the same against theft, destruction, injury, damage or loss by fire, lightning, earthquake or any casualty whatsoever. Provided, however, that if my Executors should see fit to insure said property against either or any such casualties, they may pay the cost of such insurance out of my estate.

Bibliography

Baltimore in the 80's and 90's. Meredith Janvier, H. G. Roebuck & Son, 1933.

Baltimore—A Picture History 1858-1958. Francis F. Beirne, Hastings House, 1957.

Reminiscences of 30 Years in Baltimore. Dr. Lillian Welch, Norman Remington Co., 1920.

The Johns Hopkins University Register. Johns Hopkins University Press, 1897-98.

Some Accounts of the Pennsylvania Hospital of Philadelphia 1751-1938. Francis R. Packard, M.D., Eagle Press, 1938.

Nathaniel Holmes Morison. Rear Admiral Samuel Eliot Morison, Peabody Institute, 1957.

European Travel for Women. Mary Cadwalader Jones, Macmillan Co., London, 1900.

The Proud Possessors. Aline Saarinen, Random House, 1958.

The Third Rose: Gertrude Stein and her World. John Malcolm Brinnin, Little, Brown, 1959.

The A-B-C of Aesthetics. Leo Stein, Boni & Liveright, 1927.

Appreciation: painting, poetry and prose. Leo Stein, Crown Publishers, 1947.

Journey into the Self. Letters, papers, journals of Leo Stein, Crown Publishers, 1950.

Last Operas and Plays. Gertrude Stein, Rinehart, 1949.

When This you see, remember me: Gertrude Stein in Person, W. G. Rogers, Rinehart, 1948.

The Flowers of Friendship. Donald C. Gallup, Alfred Knopf, 1953.

Gertrude Stein. Elizabeth Sprigge, Hamilton, 1957.

The Autobiography of Alice B. Toklas. Gertrude Stein, Harcourt, Brace & World, 1933.

Three Lives. Gertrude Stein, The Modern Library, 1933.

Gertrude Stein:Form and Intelligibility. Rosalind Miller, Exposition Press, 1949.

The Alice B. Toklas Cook Book. Harper & Row, 1954.

Composition as Explanation. Gertrude Stein, Hogarth Press, 1926, London.

Lectures in America. Gertrude Stein, Random House, 1935.

Selected Writings of Gertrude Stein. Edited by Carl Van Vechten, Random House, 1946.

Matisse. Henry McBride, Alfred A. Knopf, 1930.

Matisse—His Art and his Public. Alfred Barr, Museum of Modern Art, 1951.

Homage to Matisse. Yale Literary Magazine, 1955.

The Cone Collection of Baltimore. Published by Etta Cone, 1934, Baltimore, with an introduction by Dr. George Boas.

Handbook to the Cone Collection. Introduction by Mrs.

BIBLIOGRAPHY

Adelyn D. Breeskin, 1955, published by Baltimore
Museum.
The Cone Collection: Modern French Painting. Clive
Bell, Johns Hopkins Press, 1951.

Sources and Credits

The following material is drawn from the archives of the Baltimore Museum; and permission to use and cite this material is gratefully acknowledged:

letters from Gertrude, Michael, Sarah, and Leo Stein to the Cone sisters;

letters written to Etta Cone by Dr. Claribel Cone and a few of Miss Cone's replies;

letters from Henri Matisse and Madame Duthuit to Etta Cone; these letters were translated for this book by Miss Emily Taylor;

accounts of the European trips of 1901 and 1903 with the Steins, as well as the stay in Paris of 1901, from Etta Cone's journals;

Miss Etta Cone's personal account book of 1905-06, which gives the dates of her first visits to the Picasso studio, as well as the record of her purchases; information on the date of the Cone sisters' initial visit to the Matisse home at 19 Quai Street, on Michel in the winter of 1906, and on the first purchase of a Matisse water color and drawing, from the same source.

Dr. Cone's account of attending the vernissage of 1905 Salon d'Automne;

photographs of the Cone apartments, of the Cone sisters, and of Michael and Sarah Stein.

The permission of the Gertrude Stein estate and the Gertrude Stein Collection at the Yale University Library to use quotations and to reproduce original photographs as follows is gratefully acknowledged:

letters written by Etta Cone to Gertrude Stein dating from 1903 to 1936;

the June 23, 1924, exchange of letters between Gertrude Stein and Etta Cone concerning the possibility of selling the manuscript of *Three Lives*. Etta Cone's letter was printed with an incorrect date (1909) and consequent misinterpretation in *The Flowers of Friendship* by Donald Gallup (Alfred A. Knopf, Inc., 1953). The correct dating and sequence of the letters in this book has been accomplished with the kind co-operation of Mr. Gallup;

the photograph of the Cone sisters with Gertrude Stein in Florence, 1904;

the profile Gertrude Stein wrote of the Cone sisters is titled "Two Women" and was published in the "Contact Collection of Contemporary Writers" in 1925 by Robert McAlmon. It is printed here from an original typescript in the Yale University Library. The manuscript in Gertrude Stein's handwriting, written in a school notebook, is also in the library. Various parenthetical directions by Miss Stein to herself sug-

gesting the information she could draw on for the profile indicate how well the author knew the Cone family
background. In asides, written in a smaller handwriting than the main text, Miss Stein wrote:

> tell about the other—with them, then duties and
> how they did them, what effort they had when they
> were traveling, how they quarreled, how they spent
> money, how they each had what they wanted,
> Martha when she wanted it, Ada when she was go-
> ing to want it. Stinginess, buying scarves. Heaping
> things, patting hair, a little crazy, dress-making
> scenes, friends of each. Pleasing anybody. Etta and
> no father no mother. Sex in both . . .

The next aside reads:

> Complete description of the two, each one of them,
> Etta family father and mother, Ida, house, Saturday
> evenings, Hetty, Claribel, Sidney, Clarence, Hor-
> tense, etc. Amy, Carrie Gutman, Claribel, career
> . . . and the young men, reading, Flexner, sex, Ger-
> mans, *bon marche*, boxes, science, photographs,
> Etta, Brother Mosey.
> Describe Ada, the whole family, youth, Ida, broth-
> ers, art, flattery, family, lady, etc.
> Go on with their lives, and then needs for young
> womanhood. How being old is saying what you used
> to feel.
> Go on with each one of them younger and older
> and old. And other people and then a short narra-

tive of how much money they had, what they did with it, to when they left it. Their family and their relatives the number of brothers and sisters they had . . . and how their mother and father died . . . and how they were afraid of heart compaint and how Bertha had it.

Miss Stein began the profile using the sisters' names and then gave Etta the name "Ada," Claribel "Martha."

A selection of early Cone family letters was loaned to the author by Mrs. Sidney Berney, Baltimore, Maryland.

The photograph of the Cone brothers and early photographs of the Cone sisters were kindly loaned to the author by Mrs. Julius W. Cone, Greensboro, North Carolina.

The photograph of the Cones on elephant-back in India was kindly loaned to the author by Edward T. Cone of Princeton, New York.

Various photographs of the Cone sisters were kindly loaned to the author by Mrs. Lily Schwarz, Baltimore, Maryland, and Miss Nora Kaufman, Baltimore, Maryland.

The photograph of the 1901 graduating class of Johns Hopkins Medical School is courtesy of the William Welch Medical Library of the Johns Hopkins University.

Regarding the various claims of the Stein family on the purchase of Henri Matisse's "Femme au Chapeau":

Leo Stein says in his book *Appreciation: painting, poetry, and prose* (Crown Publishers, 1947) that he had purchased "Femme au Chapeau." Madame Margot Matisse Duthuit, daughter of the painter, supported Leo Stein's claims in an interview with the author.

Gertrude Stein, in her *Autobiography of Alice B. Toklas* (Random House, 1933) says that she bought the painting. Miss Toklas, in an interview with the author, reiterated Miss Stein's statement.

Henri Matisse, writing in *Transition* in 1935, said:

> Madame Michel Stein, whom Gertrude Stein neglects to mention, was the really intelligently sensitive member of the family. Leo Stein thought very highly of her because she possessed a sensibility which awakened the same thing in himself.

> It was Madame Michel Stein and her brother (in-law) who discussed the advisability of purchasing 'La Femme au Chapeau.' When the purchase had been made, Leo said to M. Michel Stein: 'I am going to ask you to leave it with me for I must know in detail the reasons for my preferences.'

> In the end it was M. Michel Stein who came into possession of the picture at the time when Leo, who had broken with Gertrude Stein, sold the collection.

The account of Etta Cone's typing of *Three Lives* for Gertrude Stein is from *The Autobiography of Alice B. Toklas* (Random House, 1933). All references in this work to the writings of Leo Stein were drawn from his

Appreciation: painting, poetry, and prose (Crown Publishers, 1947). Permission to cite material from these books is gratefully acknowledged.

The statement by Margot Matisse Duthuit, "The friendship and buying of the Cones began in 1906 and it was constant and steady thereafter," was made to the author in an interview.

All mention of paintings purchased by the Cone sisters at the Bernheim-Jeune galleries is based on information the author obtained directly from gallery records. Prices of paintings in dollars have been calculated on the basis of then current franc valuation. The author wishes to express her deep appreciation to M. Michel Dauberville and M. Jean Dauberville for their generous cooperation.

Information on the price Dr. Claribel Cone paid Pablo Picasso for her portrait in 1922 was obtained September, 1960, by Siegfried Rosengart during a visit with the artist.

It has been stated by John Malcolm Brinnin in *The Third Rose* that Gertrude Stein gave the gouache of Leo Stein to Etta Cone. Alice B. Toklas told the author in an interview that this was not the case; the painting was sold by Miss Stein to Miss Cone in 1932.

Information on the contemporary reviews of the 1905 Salon d'Automne, as well as that on the collection of Dr. Albert C. Barnes, is drawn from Alfred Barr's *Matisse: His Art and His Public* (Museum of Modern Art, 1951).

Information on the Shchukin collection in Leningrad is derived from a few art folios published by the Soviet

317

Government when the paintings were part of the Museum of Modern Western Art. The count of the Matisse paintings in the Shchukin collection is taken from Alfred Barr's book.

Information on the collections in the Baltimore Museum is from *A Century of Baltimore Collecting* and *A Picture Book—200 Objects in the Baltimore Museum of Art,* published by the Baltimore Museum.

Information on Etta Cone's will is taken from the published text of the will; facts and figures on the building of the Cone wing are from the files of the Baltimore Sun, courtesy of A. D. Emmart.

Information on the dispersal of the Sarah and Michael Stein art collection is drawn from Aline B. Saarinen's *The Proud Possessors* (Random House, 1958).

Information on the eventual bequeathal of Gertrude Stein's paintings is from John Malcolm Brinnin's *The Third Rose* (Little, Brown, 1959).

Mrs. Adelyn D. Breeskin, who was so helpful with this book, resigned as director of the Baltimore Museum in June, 1962, to become first director of the new Washington Gallery of Modern Art. Charles B. Parkhurst has succeeded Mrs. Breeskin at the Baltimore Museum.

Acknowledgments

The author wishes to acknowledge her appreciation to Dr. Florence Bamberger, Jean Barrett, Mr. and Mrs. Sidney Berney, Dr. George Boas, Mrs. Adelyn D. Breeskin, George and Tema Caylor, Mr. and Mrs. Ben Cone, Mrs. Ceasar Cone, Edward T. Cone, Harold Cone, Mrs. Laura W. Cone, Mr. and Mrs. Sydney Cone, Vivian Cooper, Michel and Jean Dauberville of Bernheim-Jeune, Arthur Drexler, Margot Matisse Duthuit, A. D. Emmart, Dudley Frasier, Philip Friedman, Donald Gallup, Suzanne Gladden, Betty Green, Maurice Grosser, Richard Guggenheimer, Mrs. Walter A. Haas, Ernest Hauser, Ellen Berney Hirschland, Mrs. Victor Jelenko, Maisie Johnson, Nora Kaufman, Mrs. Barbara Kaye, Mr. and Mrs. Samuel Kirkham, Mrs. Janet Koudelka, Leon Kroll, David Lan Bar, Dr. and Mrs. M. J. Levy, Jr., Mrs. Frances Lowenstein, Mrs. Herbert McAneny, Gloria McDonald, Herman Maril, Pierre Matisse, Richard Moses, May Nice, Madame Gabrielle Osorio, Philip Perlman, Pablo Picasso, Louis Pollack, Gus and Sam Pollack, Reginald Pollack, David Rosen, Angela Rosengart, Siegfried Rosengart, Dr. Gertrude Rosenthal, Aline B.

319

Saarinen, Mrs. Irma Claribel Scharff, Lily Schwarz, Hannah Seitzick, M.D., Doris Shalley, Mary and Bill Smela, Aaron Sopher, Herman and Ida Stanger, Beatrice Stein Steigmuller, Gertrude Stroop, Emily Taylor, Alice B. Toklas, Grace Turnbull, Elinor Ulman, Mrs. Joseph Ulman, Paul Vallotton, Beverly Williams.

The author wishes to thank the following library staffs: Yale University Library, Princeton University Library, New York Public Library, Museum of Modern Art, Metropolitan Museum, Baltimore Museum Library, Peabody Institute, Welch Medical Library of the Johns Hopkins University, Medical and Chirurgical Library in Baltimore, Women's Medical College of Pennsylvania.